CONTENTS

Feminist Review is published three times a year by a collective based in London, with help from women and groups all over the UK.

The collective: Annie Whitehead, AnnMarie Wolpe, Catherine Hall, Clara Connolly, Cora Kaplan, Dot Griffiths, Erica Carter, Jane Parkin, Kum-Kum Bhavnani, Loretta Loach, Lynne Segal, Mary McIntosh, Mica Nava, Naila Kabeer, Sue O'Sullivan.

The group that prepared this special issue also included Mary MacLeod and Esther Saraga.

Correspondence and advertising
For contributions and all other correspondence please write to:
Feminist Review, 11 Carleton Gardens, Brecknock Road, London N19 5AQ.
For subscriptions and advertising please write to:
David Polley, Methuen & Co Ltd, 11 New Fetter Lane, London EC4P 4EE

Contributions
Feminist Review is happy to discuss proposed work with intending authors at an early stage. We need copy to come to us in our house style with references complete and in the right form. We can supply you with a style sheet. Please send in 4 copies plus the original (5 copies in all). In cases of hardship 2 copies will do.

Bookshop distribution in the USA
Inland Book Company Inc., 22 Hemingway Avenue, East Haven CT 06512, USA.

Typeset by Scarborough Typesetting Services
Printed in Great Britain at the
University Press, Cambridge

ISSN number 0141-7789

NOTICEBOARD

Survivors of Child Sexual Abuse

At the First International Conference on Incest and Related Problems held at the Irchel University, Zurich, on 10–12 August, the following was read out by Survivors of Child Sexual Abuse:

> Incest is not a THEORY – it is FACTS
> DON'T give us pills – give us alternatives
> Punish the CRIMINAL – NOT the victim
> DON'T tell us what to do – GIVE US THE MONEY TO DO IT
> Whilst the victim needs a witness – INCEST REMAINS LEGAL
> Make homes SAFE – REMOVE THE ABUSER
> STOP Incest – START telling the TRUTH
> Blaming MOTHERS is too easy – BLAME THE ABUSER
> Incest is a Life Sentence for US – It should be FOR THEM
> Rape a Child – YOU RAPE YOUR FUTURE

Demands were also made that governments change the laws in favour of the child who has been abused, and that effective implementation of these laws is monitored; that self-help organizations and voluntary groups working in the interest of the child are given resources and the means with which to do the studies and research that still is desperately needed – so that education can happen; and that all professionals are trained by organizations such as those that are currently working around these issues, in particular those who work within the legal system, take initiatives in the fields of information, education and prevention, and that any initiatives taken by these are effectively monitored. For further information write to LESPOP, 4 Wild Court, London WC2B 5AU.

Lesbian Custody

Rights of Women have produced a new Lesbian Custody leaflet and are at present putting together a resource pack dealing with this issue. Both will be available from 52–54 Featherstone Street, London EC1Y 8RT at a cost of 50p each.

New Journal

The National Women's Studies Association (NWSA) is publishing a new interdisciplinary, multicultural feminist journal, the *NWSA Quarterly Journal* and is actively soliciting articles and reviews of interest to women's studies researchers and trainers. Prospective contributors should write to Mary Jo Wagner, Editor, Center for Women's Studies, 207 Dulles Hall, 230 West 17th Avenue, Ohio State University, Columbus, Ohio 43701, USA.

Leadership and Power

This year's National Women's Studies Association annual conference will be held on 22–26 June 1988 around the issue of 'Leadership and Power: Women's Alliances for Social Change'. For more information contact Lois Graven, Department of Professional Development, 315 Pillsbury Drive S. E., University of Minnesota, Minneapolis, MN 55455-0139, USA.

Call for Papers: Women, Family, State and Economy in Africa

The editors of this special issue of *Signs* seek papers and research reports based on recent field and/or archival work that consider the interactive relationship between changes in the lives of specific groups, classes or communities of African women and one of the following: 1) changing family composition, structure and well-being; 2) state policies and interventions as they impact women's lives, activities and options; 3) economic changes and development, whether formulated in the context of regional, national or international forces. *Signs* is committed to including a substantial body of materials that reflect the significant scholarly work being undertaken by African women, and welcomes unpublished material as well as new English translations of material published in other languages. Papers must be received by 30 September 1988 at *Signs*, 207 East Duke Building, Duke University, Durham, NC 27708, USA.

Organizational Psychology — National Women at Work Conference

This international working conference for feminist researchers, writers, lecturers and practitioners in industry, commerce, HE/FE, consultancy and the professions will enable women-centred decisionmakers and administrators to explore common themes, examine inherent conflicts and to look at our own theoretical developments and practical strategies in employee relations, systems analysis, management, bureaucracy and organizational behaviours. For details write to Sandra Oliver, Faculty Office, Thames Polytechnic, Oakfield Lane, Dartford, Kent DA1 2SZ.

Apologies to Lesley Doyal

The *Feminist Review* collective sends sincere apologies to Lesley Doyal both for misspelling her name and for giving inaccurate information in the biographical note to her article in *Feminist Review* No. 27. Lesley has recently taken up a position in the Department of Nursing, Health and Applied Social Studies at Bristol Polytechnic; she was also one of the founders of WHIC, the Women's Health Information Centre. We deeply regret the mistakes, and the embarrassment caused.

INTRODUCTION TO AN ISSUE:
Family Secrets as Public Drama

Mary McIntosh

In the introduction to *Feminist Review*'s book, *Sexuality* (1987), we referred to the emergence as major political issues of violence against women, rape and child abuse, in the wake of feminist concern as expressed through Women's Aid, Rape Crisis lines and Incest Survivors' groups. During 1987 the issue of child sexual abuse exploded in Britain in an even more dramatic way, triggered first by Esther Rantzen's launch of a telephone help-line, ChildLine, on national television (on 30 October 1986) and boosted by the press exploitation of a dispute in Cleveland about a dramatic leap in the number of children being taken into care suspected of being victims of buggery. Rantzen and Cleveland represented a moral crusade – however ill-judged and poorly planned – and its retrogressive backlash. Between them they have forced a particular formulation of the question of child sexual abuse into the public domain.[1]

The formulation of the question is not one that feminists would have chosen. Perhaps its most remarkable feature is the absence of the perpetrator as a recognizable character in the drama. There are 'parents', ungendered and acting in couples, readily endowed with all the rosy lineaments of the myth of modern classless parenthood, and there are 'children', also often ungendered, and of indeterminate age. The key problems in the drama revolve around these children. How many of them are there and are there more than before? How and to whom can they speak and can they be believed? Can they be trained to protect themselves or do they need protecting and, if so, how and by whom? All of these are important questions, but surely not the only ones that need to be debated. Surrounding these central protagonists is a supporting cast of character actors: the stressed and perplexed (or empire-building) social workers, the fanatical (or crusading) paediatrician, the cynical (or realistic) police surgeon, the Labour MP in search of populist local credibility, the harassed help-line workers, the ordinary teachers and doctors in need of clear guidelines, the puzzled parent who dare not cuddle his child, and so on.

The Esther Rantzen scenario was much looser and had fewer of these stock characters. Everything centred on the children, whatever form of abuse they might have suffered. They might have been frightened by a flasher, touched up on a train, buggered by a school bully, raped by an uncle or forced to masturbate their father (experiences which may well have a lot in common, and none of which is necessarily trivial). There was no clearly defined antagonist – and as a result, the plot lacked dramatic tension (which therefore came to centre around the organizational problems of ChildLine). For this reason, child sexual abuse might well have been a nine-day wonder as far as the media were concerned if it had not been for the backlash, in the form of the lavishly staged production in Cleveland. At the time this article is being written, in the late summer of 1987 when the public inquiry is still under way, it is impossible to know what really went on in the various agencies in Cleveland, let alone in the families whose children were taken to 'a place of safety', or how it was all affected by the publicity. All that we can know at present is how it was formulated as a public issue by the media. What the backlash, as presented in the media, did was to focus the drama on The Family, to say that the trendy concern about child sexual abuse was an intrusion on the normal intimacy between parents and children: snooping busybodies invoking the interventionist state to subvert the natural rights of parents. Here were antagonists worthy of classic tragedy: not the abuser and the abused, but The Family and The State.

Another notable feature of the new formulation of the question is the way in which it has displaced all of the earlier ways of talking about overlapping questions. The concern with child sexual abuse lies, in a sense, at the confluence of two distinct historical streams, one of them concerned with cruelty to children, mainly within the home or the family, and the other concerned with sexual relations with children, mainly outside the family.

There is, of course, a very venerable *name* for this point of confluence – incest – but it is a name that had become almost empty of social content. A law against incest (by men) was first introduced in England and Wales in 1908, after more than two decades of pressure from enlightened sources like Beatrice Webb, the Housing Commission of 1884 (concerned about the way that overcrowded housing conditions fostered immorality) and the National Society for the Prevention of Cruelty to Children (Weeks, 1981: 31). Incest was seen from the outside, as a problem of the working class.

Yet during the early 1980s, the Criminal Law Revision Committee was able to discuss the possibility of abolishing the law of incest with scarcely a reference to any social realities. Incest seemed to be a regressive but fairly harmless subcultural pattern in some rural areas, or one pathological feature among others of a deviant problem family, or

else a rare, and possibly romantic, relationship between an adult sister and brother. There was some minimal discussion of whether to extend the law of incest to cover non-blood relationships and acts other than intercourse, to take account of perceived changes in the family and in sexual practices, but given the fact that incest, as at present legally defined takes no account of age, and given the problems of defining the wider relationships involved (should stepfatherhood, common-law stepfatherhood, stepbrotherhood and half-brotherhood be included?), it was felt that the ordinary law of sexual assaults on minors was adequate. The whole discussion was much more academic and low key than it could conceivably be today.

Over the past hundred years or so, public anxiety about the sexual abuse of children has erupted intermittently into a highly charged 'moral panic'.[2] Jeffrey Weeks has described 1885 as 'an *annus mirabilis* of sexual politics' (Weeks, 1981: 87). It was the year in which W. T. Stead produced his exposé of child prostitution in London, 'The Maiden Tribute of Modern Babylon'. Social purity campaigners, who by that time had been joined by feminists such as Josephine Butler, combined with socialists and freethinkers in expressing outrage. A quarter of a million people demonstrated in Hyde Park demanding that the age of consent be raised from thirteen to sixteen. As a result of the outcry provoked by 'The Maiden Tribute', the Criminal Law Amendment Act was rushed through Parliament. This is now, perhaps, best remembered for its 'Labouchère Amendment' which criminalized 'acts of gross indecency' between men; but it also had provision for suppressing brothels and it established the current age of consent for girls at sixteen.

The image of child sexual abuse of 1885 was that of the helpless victim sold as a 'five pound virgin' to satisfy the jaded lusts of a perverted aristocrat. It was a mercenary, loveless, heterosexual event across a wide chasm of age, power and social class. As in 1987, the focus was on the vulnerability of the victim and her need for protection, rather than on the character of the abuser. Quite different was the focal image in the paedophilia scandal of the late 1970s, whose impetus was the 'coming out' and claim to liberation of men, mainly gay men, who were sexually interested in the young.

The paedophile movement sprang out of the gay liberation movement, and also threatened to wreck that movement by dividing it on the issue of 'man-boy love'. The North American Man/Boy Love Association, formed in Boston in 1978, and the British Paedophile Information Exchange (PIE), started in the mid-1970s, argued that age-of-consent laws deny children's sexuality and children's right to self-expression. They presented an image of sexual relations between men and boys as natural, loving and reciprocal and as stigmatized only by an unhealthy attitude to sex and a repressive morality. Their language was that of the sexual libertarianism of the 1960s, familiar to the women's and gay movements.

The backlash against PIE, and the witch-hunting of its spokesperson, Tom O'Carroll, was probably more significant and sustained than the organization itself. PIE became the occasion for the most venomous outrage against 'perverts' of all kinds and for the perpetuation of the myth that homosexuals are paedophiles and paedophiles are homosexual. In all the flood of invective around the natural versus the perverse, the issues that feminists wanted to debate – can sex between those who are unequal in power ever be justified? how can children's rights to freedom of expression be reconciled with protecting them against exploitation? why is it nearly always men rather than women who want sex with children? – were totally submerged.

Now, less than a decade later, adult-child sex has again erupted as an issue but this time the focus has returned to the child, with the abuser a shadowy figure in the background. Where the issue around paedophilia was 'should perverts be allowed to speak, write or even exist?' – or at best 'perversion versus naturalness' – the issue today is posed as 'should children, or professionals, be allowed to accuse parents of abuse without cast-iron proof?' What is extraordinary about the history of public issues, as created by and responded to in the mass media, is the extent of amnesia about earlier formulations of issues around the same thing. The campaigners of PIE and the peddlers of 'kiddy porn' have disappeared as if they had never been. In the feverish search for 'news', the media foreswear learning from the old, and the public is invited to engage with a new problem, equipped only with the weapons of common sense and a pristine morality. Yet the media formulations of issues do have an impact on social policy. The professions and agencies that work in the field may evolve a gradually maturing knowledge and understanding only to find that a national moral panic alters the climate within which they must operate and sends them off in a new direction.

Such a zig-zag course has often been noted in the history of social policy in relation to cruelty to children. Here again, a particular instance of child abuse, usually one in which a child dies, can be the occasion of a moral panic that turns public policy about and sets it on a new tack. At one extreme is the principle developed by the 'child savers' in the late nineteenth century that the well-being of children is a public concern and that state and other agencies have a right to intervene and remove a child from its parents where cruelty and neglect are suspected. Although nominally a classless principle, this in effect has meant that bourgeois state and other agencies have kept an eye on working-class parents, setting minimal standards for good parenting that corresponded to bourgeois ideals and needs. At the other extreme is the view that it is in the child's best interests for it to remain with its natural parents, even if they are very unsatisfactory, or with a permanent substitute family: temporary removal or institutional care are seen as the very last resort. This pro-family view gained support in the post-war period with the popularization of John Bowlby's ideas about 'maternal deprivation' and of psychoanalytic ideas about the importance of relations with parents for child development. Institutional care lost favour and the children's homes that remained were broken down into cottages with 'house parents'. The newspaper publicity surrounding the tragic death of a foster child, Denis O'Neil, in 1946, set the seal on the policy that was to dominate the next thirty years, in which the preference was for leaving children with their natural parents wherever possible and developing local social services to keep an eye on them and offer support.

During this period, meanwhile, the medical profession was developing the concept of the 'battered child', a term first used in the United States in 1961. The idea was that doctors could recognize a syndrome of typical injuries and if there was a history of previous injuries and no plausible explanation was offered it could be assumed that the child was being battered by its parents. Medical thinking and practice developed during the 1960s without much publicity; the preference was for bringing in the social services rather than the police when battering was suspected. When there was wider public aware-ness, from 1968 onwards, it tended, according to Nigel Parton (1985), to be informed by the views of the influential NSPCC Battered Child Research Unit, which saw battering as a 'cry for help' in a disturbed family and recommended an emphasis on preventive work. Parton says:

> While the 'protection of the child' was seen as crucial, it was felt that this could generally be done in terms of rehabilitation for the whole family.
> (Parton, 1985:67)

In 1973, however, a new scandal arose around the death of seven-year-old Maria Colwell, beaten to death by her stepfather after social workers had reluctantly allowed her mother to reclaim her from foster care. The presumption in favour of the natural mother, as against the admittedly good and caring home provided for many years by the foster parents, led to a tragic outcome. The moral panic that ensued incorporated apocalyptic themes about social collapse into a violent society as well as a critique of social workers as ineffectual to deal with the real evils threatening the 'English way of life'. Maria Colwell's death, the public inquiry that followed it and the moral panic that they occasioned mark the beginning of child abuse – at first termed Non-Accidental Injury (NAI) by the professionals involved – as a major object of social welfare mobilization. Procedures for dealing with suspected cases, and especially for notification, liaison between different agencies and case conferences and area review committees, were all consolidated. The police were involved, but criminal proceed-ings were rarely used against abusers. Everyone lived in fear of 'another Maria Colwell' in their caseload, and indeed there were a number of similar cases, with ensuing public inquiries and pilloried social workers, during the following decade. After each scandal, social service depart-ments tended to play safe for a while and 'when in doubt' remove the child but, in general, they continued to favour keeping children in their families, despite the fact that they were under-resourced to carry out effective preventive work. By the beginning of the 1980s, central registers of children 'at risk' began to include children thought to be at risk of physical neglect and emotional and sexual abuse, as well as physical injury.

Meanwhile, however, the social services were increasingly recruiting among people who had been influenced as students by radical deviancy theory, by feminism and by a form of anti-racism that emphasized a resistance to cultural imperialism. Such radical social workers found themselves in a contradictory situation, having been brought up in the belief that 'social workers are social policemen'. They could readily see that social work 'intervention' into the lives of families, although conducted in the name of the best interests of the child, was also a form of policing of the lower orders on behalf of a bourgeois state. Social workers tell mothers how they should behave; they judge white working-class people by middle-class standards and Black people by white middle-class standards; and in the case of suspected child abuse they have the power to impose their norms and to punish people by taking their children away. At the same time, some local councils, in London and elsewhere, had people of similar politics sitting on their social services committees, and anti-racism was a major issue in many boroughs. Along with this, in the early 1980s, there was a certain amount of civil liberties agitation on behalf of mothers who had had their children taken into care in some crisis and were finding it impossible to get them back. All of these factors combined to produce a hands-off policy in some social services departments, keeping a watching brief on children 'at risk' but often reluctant to take children into care because they were mistrustful of their own white middle-class judgement.

Feminists are bound to be rather ambivalent about this kind of policy. Many of us would argue that, if the battle lines are to be drawn up as State versus Family, we should side with the State, even with a white bourgeois state. Black women as well as white have wanted to call in the police to protect us against a violent husband, though we have preferred to set up our own refuges and networks; and we have wanted an independent right to social security benefits rather than dependence on a well-paid husband. Most feminists believe that a class consciousness or an anti-racism that uses a patriarchal family as its resistance cell has nothing to offer to women.[3] On the other hand, such simplistic polarities do not correspond to many poor women's and Black women's experiences: social workers are from another and more powerful world and you do well to keep out of their clutches. Lesbian mothers of all classes have the same experience, but middle-class ones have more escape routes.

One of the things that we have learnt in the past decade is that the state apparatuses need not be monolithically white, Eurocentric and bourgeois. A Black social worker informed by Afro-Caribbean feminism may intervene in a Black family in a very different way from a white social worker. The solution may not be a hands-off policy, but the development of more specific resources for – and by – specific groups. Black and Asian women's centres, for instance, can provide appropriate support and a child from an embattled racially oppressed group may feel able to disclose sexual abuse to one of her own people where it would be treachery to do so to a white person. Such projects may also be able to avoid police involvement, which can be particularly problematic for Black people. In other words, the same arguments apply to violence and to sexual abuse as apply to mental health: as well as white professionals becoming more aware of the risks of racism in their diagnostic practices, it is necessary to have specific projects directed towards each group. A parallel might be the fact that in the Netherlands there are lesbian and gay mental health services – surely the best way of ensuring that breaking with normative heterosexuality neither gets you labelled as criminal or mentally ill, nor means that your genuine mental health needs go unmet.

In 1985 a spate of deaths of very young children, of whom Tyra Henry and Jasmine Beckford were to become the most celebrated, sparked off another moral panic. There were powerful elements of racism and of fear of a white underclass (shades of the 'dangerous classes' that haunted the nineteenth-century bourgeoisie), admixed with the usual dread of social decay and the disintegration of the family, which is portrayed as the well-spring of all that is moral and caring in society. In these cases the children were living with their natural mothers and, as in the Maria Colwell scandal, the social workers were castigated for their inactivity, their culpable failure to intervene. Only two years later, in stark contrast, we have the spectacle of the social workers and paediatricians of Cleveland pilloried for overzealous intervention and for lacking due respect for the rights of parents. Once again, there is the extraordinary amnesia of the media: this new drama is offered for our entertainment as if it were the first of its kind, rather than an example of an all-too-familiar genre. We are never invited to refer back or to make comparisons, let alone to strike a balance or to learn from history.

We are putting together this special issue of *Feminist Review* in the ebb tide of the most recent moral panic, the first to combine the two currents of adult-child sex and cruelty to children. By the time it is published, such is the brevity of the 'issue-attention cycle', Cleveland will be stale news but we do not apologise for jumping on the wrong bandwagon, and too late. For what we aim to do is to help rescue child sexual abuse from the media, where it will be alternately caricatured and forgotten, and establish it in a space where there can be a feminist agenda. There is, after all, a many-sided and problematic reality behind all the media hype. Feminists were the first to recognize it and the challenges that it poses. It deserves a rather longer attention-span than the mass media will ever give it.

It is hard for us, though, to escape the agenda that we have been offered. The articles in this issue are, on the whole, feminist interventions in debates that are on-going outside of feminism, though we hope that they will be part of the groundwork for debates *within* feminism and for the establishment of a feminist policy agenda. For instance, I have commented on the absence of the abuser as a rounded character in the currently popular drama of child sexual abuse. We are able to do little in this issue of *Feminist Review* to remedy this; but we can point the way forward and hope that the new flowering of publications on masculinity will shed some light on why so many men abuse their own and other children in this way. Similarly, I have commented on the way in which the drama has become centred on the family and earlier dramas about paedophilia and dangerous strangers have been pushed aside. Yet we too concentrate our attention here on abuse within households, and households within Britain, on the whole. The wider world of child prostitution, the international traffic in children, sex tourism and child pornography (all coolly, yet chillingly, discussed by Judith Ennew, 1986) may be numerically smaller, but it provides the context and surely some of the imagery and motivation for domestic sexual abuse.

Feminism may not have set the agenda as far as the mass media are concerned, but, as several of the articles here reveal, it is having a considerable – if uneven – impact on local policy in many places and also in professional arenas. It was the women's movement, starting with small beginnings in consciousness-raising in the 1970s, that enabled the breaking of the silence, the formation of Incest Survivors' groups and the whole opening up of the question of child sexual abuse. Rape Crisis centres and other women's organizations have played a vital part in bringing the issue to light and they continue to do feminist work in the front line. In some localities, women's groups are taking the initiative in the development of local training, awareness and practice; we publish examples from Glasgow and Norwich. And feminists working in the schools and the social services are beginning to find ways to influence what goes on there. We hope that this issue of *Feminist Review* will help to strengthen and extend these activities.

Notes

Mary McIntosh teaches sociology at the University of Essex and is a member of the *Feminist Review* collective.

1 Two provocative books on the way in which child abuse has been formulated as a social problem are Barbara Nelson's *Making an Issue of Child Abuse* (1984), about the United States, and Nigel Parton's *The Politics of Child Abuse* (1985), about Britain.

2 Nigel Parton (1985: ch.4) has used the concept of moral panic, as elaborated by Hall and others (1978), in an interesting discussion of the social reaction to the death of Maria Colwell.

3 Yet some, like Jane Humphries (1977), have argued that the family has played an important part in British working-class history, creating and transmitting class consciousness, motivating political struggle and thereby benefiting women as well as men; and others, like Hazel Carby (1982), have seen the Black family as a prime source of political and cultural resistance to

racism. Michèle Barrett and I have taken issue with both Humphries (Barrett and McIntosh, 1980) and Carby (Barrett and McIntosh, 1985).

References

BARRETT, Michèle and MCINTOSH, Mary (1980) 'The "Family Wage": Some Problems for Socialists and Feminists' *Capital and Class* No. 11, Summer 1980.

BARRETT, Michèle and MCINTOSH, Mary (1985) 'Ethnocentrism and Socialist-feminist Theory' *Feminist Review* No. 20, Summer 1985.

CARBY, Hazel (1982) 'White Woman Listen! Black Feminism and the Boundaries of Sisterhood' in CENTRE FOR CONTEMPORARY CULTURAL STUDIES, 1982.

CENTRE FOR CONTEMPORARY CULTURAL STUDIES (1982) *The Empire Strikes Back: Race and Racism in Seventies Britain* London: Hutchinson.

ENNEW, Judith (1986) *The Sexual Exploitation of Children* Cambridge: Polity Press.

FEMINIST REVIEW (1987) editors *Sexuality: A Reader* London: Virago Press.

HALL, S., CRICHTER, C., JEFFERSON, T., CLARKE, J. and ROBERTS, B. (1978) *Policing the Crisis: Mugging, the State and Law and Order* London: Macmillan.

HUMPHRIES, Jane (1977) 'Class Struggle and the Persistence of the Working-class Family' *Cambridge Journal of Economics* Vol. 1 no. 3.

NELSON, Barbara J. (1984) *Making an Issue of Child Abuse: Political Agenda Setting for Social Problems* Chicago: University of Chicago Press.

PARTON, Nigel (1985) *The Politics of Child Abuse* London: Macmillan.

WEEKS, Jeffrey (1981) *Sex, Politics and Society: The Regulation of Sexuality since 1800* Harlow: Longman.

CHALLENGING THE ORTHODOXY:
Towards a Feminist Theory and Practice

Mary MacLeod and Esther Saraga

> We need to have confidence in our ability to read and interpret. Rather
> than believe in 'experts' who imply they know it all, we must look for the
> gaps and the hidden agendas. If knowledge and power go hand in hand, it
> is the responsibility of feminists both to acquire knowledge and to
> transform it. (Cameron and Frazer 1987: xv)

In all the storm of words about child sexual abuse, there has been a
deafening silence on why it happens. This is strange. For, finding a
meaning is a central concern of everyone touched by child sexual abuse.
Why did it happen?, why did he do it? are questions which obsessively
preoccupy sufferers of abuse and their relatives. The abusers who can
accept some responsibility for their actions also struggle to find
answers.

Child sexual abuse is also at the centre of many ideological debates,
bringing together as it does sexuality and the family; yet, the debates
seldom address why child sexual abuse occurs. Rather, anyone with an
issue to explore or a point to make attaches child sexual abuse to it as the
clinching argument. Seabrooke, in the *New Statesman* (1987), adopts it
to argue the debauchery of the market economy; Labour MP Stuart Bell,
the integrity of the north-east working-class family; critics and apologists of psychoanalysis use it to attack or defend; James Anderton, Chief
Constable of Greater Manchester, to argue for more repressive policing
and draconian sentencing.

Why then is there evident in political, professional and journalistic
writings, such a curious absence of discussion on why abuse occurs? The
answer should come as no surprise to feminists; it enables an avoidance
of the most glaring feature of child sexual abuse: it is something that,
overwhelmingly, men do to children. The men come from every social
class, and from all kinds of families and cultures; they are brothers,

confused

uncles, babysitters, friends, strangers, grandfathers, stepfathers and fathers. They have in common that they are men, but little else that we know. Very little attention has been paid to studying them, and none to the study of non-abusive men.

Interestingly, the focus of frantic study and hypothesis are the children who are abused, the families they come from and, more than almost anything else, the women who are their mothers. One particular theoretical approach, family dysfunction theory, has, in locating child sexual abuse in 'problem families', dominated lay and professional discourse and achieved the status of common sense. Its main attribute, certainly not logic, is the comfort it affords to the establishment and the great general public. It calms the collective anxiety about the 'family' which erupts, as in the furore over Cleveland, when the reality of sexual abuse of children within families emerges.

Though family dysfunction theory currently holds the position of orthodoxy among professionals, it is actually one of many explanations of child sexual abuse. In this article we want to look at, and offer a feminist critique of, three influential approaches: the *libertarian* view, *psychoanalysis* and *family dysfunction*, before elaborating a feminist approach. The approaches are worth exploring in some detail because they have powerfully constrained the ways that child sexual abuse is talked and thought about, and influenced the kinds of intervention and help that occur. These broad approaches are not theoretically pure; they often share assumptions, starting points and arguments. This also is not surprising, since these ideas have all developed within a very old set of discourses, within European culture, about sex, men, women, children and incest.

The furore set off by Cleveland shows us how child sexual abuse arouses a deep collective anxiety about the family: an anxiety that troubles equally the left and the right. The new wave of right-wing interest in idealizing the family merges with the anti-interventionist line of the left; the usual signposts to people trying to find a way to understand and take charge of a difficult issue are missing. There is no clear left or right line on child sexual abuse; indeed it is often hard to distinguish the politics of any piece on child sexual abuse.

However, the confusion, the contradiction, the absence of politics and the sheer difficulty of untangling the debates on an issue which has painful emotional resonances for all of us, must not deter us from attempting to articulate and impose a feminist analysis. It is time to cast a cold eye on the whole business. This is especially true for professionals, for those who choose to and those who are asked to help. Sarah Nelson, in an admirably cool book, *Incest: Fact and Myth*, says:

> The first step in designing a programme among social work, medical, legal and other agencies involves reaching a consensus on what incestuous abuse is about. That means agreeing a theory . . . decisions on how you deal with each family member depend crucially on how you theorize about them. (Nelson, 1987: 96)

There is without doubt just such a clear link between theory and practice. Practice (statutory, voluntary and therapeutic) has to be born of theory. The outstanding success of the initiatives of the women's movement (Rape Crisis, Women's Aid) on sexual violence against women and children is a testimony to this, and it is of course to the women's movement and the courage of survivors that the credit must go for publicly establishing child sexual abuse as the scandal it always was. However, feminist theory is still 'out in the cold' when it comes to the professional establishment.

The first step in agreeing a theory would seem to be establishing what child sexual abuse is and how common it is. This, however, is fraught with difficulties, and cannot precede theory. The way that experiences are understood by children themselves, and by lay and professional people, depends on the ways these events are commonly theorized and categorized. This affects the statistics and definitions, because research too is conducted in a culturally specific way. For example, the *Guardian* letter (11.8.87) on the Mori poll results which have given such a welcome boost to the forces of denial can say that sexual experiences such as 'showing/touching sex organs', 'fondling/kissing in a sensual way' and 'erotic talk/indecent suggestion/showing pornographic material' cannot and should not be included in figures for 'serious abuse'. Yet anyone who has a nodding acquaintance with casualties of child sexual abuse knows that children have been horribly traumatized by being the object of, for example, 'mere' verbal sexual abuse by their fathers. So it is not such a simple exercise to count the incidence of 'serious sexual abuse', or to define it.

Definitions

There are a number of definitions of child sexual abuse used in the literature. They vary according to the activities, and the relationship of abused child to abuser, which are included or excluded. The most widely used definition of child sexual abuse in the professional literature, usually attributed to Kempe and Kempe, but actually from Schecter and Roberge (1976) is:

> The involvement of developmentally immature children and adolescents in sexual actions which they cannot fully comprehend, to which they cannot give informed consent, and which violate the taboos of social roles. (Quoted in Kempe and Kempe, 1984: 9)

This definition has been criticized for not including the idea that force may be used, or the threat of force, and that the adult's power over the child may constitute sufficient coercive power (Ash, 1984). The inclusion of the idea that abusive acts must 'violate the taboos of social roles' also suggests that some acts are abusive only because they are not socially acceptable.

Recent research by the London Rape Crisis Centre (LRRC) has shown that the 'legal definitions of sexual offences are inadequate in representing the real pattern of violence' (LRRC, 1987: 39). This is particularly true of the crime of incest, which must involve penetration and is restricted to a particular set of family relationships. The term 'incest' has been further criticized by some feminists because it can imply mutuality or complicity, and because it underplays the sense of violation or trauma. Others, such as Herman (1981), Russell (1986) and Nelson (1987) choose to use 'incest' in a wider sense to include all abuse occurring in a familial context, or by any relative, however 'distant'. They believe that it is important to distinguish between abuse that occurs within and outside the family. Even this is problematic, though, because their terminology does not include abuse by someone like a teacher or friend of the family, who is not a relative but who is nevertheless close to the child and in a position of love, trust or responsibility.

Kelly (this volume) and Herman have suggested that it is important to include the child's subjective experience as part of the definition: abuse is not defined by what happens, but by how it is experienced. Russell takes a contrary view – that abuse is not dependent upon being experienced as such; many children may not have the knowledge or understanding to know that it is abuse. Many survivors find it difficult to apply 'such value-laden words' as 'rape' or 'sexual abuse' to their experiences (Russell, 1986: 24). Nelson (1987) and the Incest Survivors' Campaign both emphasize the dependent relationship of the child on her/his abuser, the inequality of power and the betrayal of trust.

Another problem with definition is the upper age limit of childhood, and the appropriate age of consent. British surveys usually take sixteen, the legal age of consent for heterosexuality for girls, as the upper age limit; but this is contested by those who argue the appropriateness of young adolescents having sexual experience with their peers. Some researchers therefore count experiences as abuse only if the abuser is at least five years older than the child. However, for intra-familial abuse, or any sexual experience involving an adult in a position of power in relation to the child, sixteen years is in our view too young; in fact age becomes more or less irrelevant. Nash and West (1985) found that some of the women in their survey felt that 'the cutoff point for childhood at age 16 was arbitrary and that their own sexual experiences with older men, when they were still too young to cope emotionally, should have been included' (Nash and West, 1985: 82). One example cited is of a sixteen-year-old raped by her employer while working as an au pair.

It is clear that the definition derives from theory; like all aspects of this subject, it is a matter for debate and discussion. The constant concern about finding the correct definition is another diversion from the real issue. Most adults, men and women, know perfectly well that certain actions and activities, from verbal abuse and harassment to rape, are abusive to children. We are not convinced by the 'worried' fathers who write to the Press that they no longer dare be affectionate with their daughters for fear of being accused of abuse. Most abusers know exactly what they are doing, and hence find ways of silencing the child.

We are concerned in this article with abuse that is defined in terms of three key elements: the betrayal of trust and responsibility, the abuse of power and the inability of children to consent. An assessment of trauma may be important to decisions on intervention, but it should not be part of the definition. We agree with the use of the broad definition, given by the Incest Survivors' Campaign (1981):

> The sexual molestation of a child by any person whom that child sees as a
> figure of trust or authority . . . we see the questions of age, blood
> relationship and taboo as red herrings which obscure the central issue:
> the irresponsible exploitation of children's ignorance, trust and obedience.
> Incest is the abuse of power. (Quoted in Nelson, 1987: 14)

The 'statistics'

The obsession with numbers following Cleveland is another false trail into the undergrowth. Nevertheless, we need to be prepared with information about the 'incidence studies' in order to counter the arguments that it really isn't as common as everyone is claiming, and shouldn't be taken so seriously.

We cannot say exactly how common child sexual abuse is. Different interpretations of the available statistics, plus the fact that most people have no direct access to any of the research, mean that it is very difficult to draw clear conclusions and easy to believe what we want to believe. However, as more and better research has been done over the last few years, and as more people have been prepared to listen to the findings, ideas have changed dramatically and, whatever the prevalence actually is, it *is* much more common than was ever imagined. The hairsplitting discussion of what is abuse, and what not, obscures the fact that children are constantly exposed to unacceptable sexual attentions from adult men.

Until recently research in this area was very limited, because of lack of interest and the very real problems about doing good research on such a painful, sensitive subject which is shrouded in secrecy. Early research (pre-1978) was based on small clinical samples, 'cases' that were on the files of some authority: police, social workers' or doctors'. These samples were obviously skewed, because very few incidents were ever reported to anyone.

One early exception to this focus on 'cases' was the Kinsey reports (1948, 1953), which surveyed more than 5,000 men and more than 4,000 women. No numerical data were reported for sexual contacts between boys and adults, but the survey on women did address this issue, looking at 'adult-child sexual contact'; terms like incest or sexual abuse were not used. Careful analyses of Kinsey's data suggest that 24 per cent of the women had been sexually abused before puberty; between 3 and 5.5 per cent by a family member (Russell, 1986; Herman, 1981). In *all* cases, the abuser was a man.

Work in the USA on child sexual abuse has been several years ahead of the UK. Following the feminist initiatives on rape and domestic violence during the 1970s, 'new feminist research and thinking on incest victimization finally started to surface in 1978' (Russell, 1986: 9), and several large-scale retrospective surveys have been conducted. In Britain there are two: the well-known Mori poll (Baker and Duncan, 1985) and a study by Nash and West (1985).

In order to interpret the results of these studies, which conclude that between one in ten and one in three girls have been incestuously abused, in the wider sense of that term, it is necessary to consider the issues of definition discussed earlier: is all abuse being included or only that within the family? What age limits are put upon childhood? However, these do not pose the only difficulties; some problems in research may be more or less inherent to the nature of child sexual abuse itself:

> Memory failure over time, subconscious or even deliberate blocking, and
> the rationalisation or the reinterpretation of emotive childhood events,
> render problematic the interpretation of information gathered
> retrospectively from adults. (Nash and West, 1985: 5)

How the research is carried out will have a major effect on the information obtained. Russell's study is impressive because it started from an understanding of, and sensitivity to, the nature of the phenomenon being investigated. Interviewers and respondents were matched where possible according to age, race and class. No other major study replicates this methodology.

> In summary: Some of the main methodological features that may explain
> why our survey obtained a 19-percent prevalence rate for incestuous

abuse of women of all ages include use of face to face interviews; use of a range of questions that helped to tap women's memories of experiences, some of them long repressed; avoidance of words like 'incest', 'molest', 'rape' (used only once); careful selection of interviewers who did not subscribe to the usual myths about sexual assault; and rigorous training of interviewers in both the administration of the interview schedule and education about rape and incest. (Russell, 1986: 25)

The Mori poll, which is extensively quoted in Britain, has been criticized for overestimating 'serious abuse' by not having a 'tight' enough definition. The reverse is true. The methodology failed to take account of the emotional impact on respondents of questions on sexual abuse, so that the results were bound to be an underestimate of the 'true' prevalence rate. The questions asked seem hardly likely to have encouraged disclosures. The interviewers presented respondents with a card on which was printed the following definition of sexual abuse:

A child (anyone under 16 years) is sexually abused when another person, who is sexually mature, involves the child in any activity which the other person expects to lead to their sexual arousal. This might involve intercourse, touching, exposure of the sexual organs, showing pornographic material or talking about things in an erotic way. (Baker and Duncan, 1985: 458)

They were asked whether they had had such an experience before age sixteen years, so that only experiences which fitted into this definition, which they themselves defined as abuse, were included in the survey.

The definition itself uses a lot of very specific words which might cause anxiety. The details of respondents' experiences could not be described in their own words, but had to fit into pre-chosen categories. Answers were given by choosing options from a 'multiple response format'. 'To minimize any embarrassment' respondents could answer by referring to the options by 'identifying letters' (Baker and Duncan, 1985: 458), a procedure which reduces personal experience to a category. Moreover, the formulation of the definition is grammatically loose: whose sexual arousal are we talking about?

The figures on the sexual abuse of boys are also a subject of disagreement. Those studies which looked at boys as well as girls (Finkelhor, 1979; Baker and Duncan, 1985) found that the proportion of girl to boy 'victims' is about 3: 2 when all sexual abuse is included, but that this proportion changes significantly (about 5: 1) when the figures look only at 'within family abuse', and some research suggests that boys tend to be abused within the family only if a girl is being abused (Weir, 1987: 5). Most abuse of boys, whether within or outside the family, is by heterosexual men. Here, and for similar reasons, we are likely to be dealing with an underestimate, though whether, as some people claim, there is an even greater silence on abuse of boys is impossible to say. There has certainly been a denial that boys will find adult–child sexual contact abusive; Kinsey did not even report on this. On the other hand, it is commonly argued that sexual abuse is even more damaging to boys because being passive or submissive is a greater distortion of male sexuality (Kempe and Kempe, 1984). Stereotyped thinking about boys' sexuality has done them a considerable disservice.

Some very important conclusions can be drawn from these retrospective studies. In the majority of cases, the abuse had *never* been reported to any authority, and in many cases the abuse was being disclosed for the first time to the interviewer. Race and class were not significant, with the exception of Asian women, among whom Russell (1986) found that there was significantly less incestuous abuse. While for the reasons discussed here it is difficult to give accurate incidence figures, abuse by stepfathers was proportionately much more common than abuse by biological fathers. The evidence suggests an increase in child sexual abuse during this century.

While some of these conclusions may be important in our arguments, it is, we believe, a matter of insignificance to the position taken on theory and practice how *many* children are sexually fondled, masturbated, raped or 'merely' flashed at. Much more important than establishing a prevalence rate is agreeing a set of rules about what is permissible and what is not.

Don't women sexually abuse too?

The first step in establishing a theory is, then, a recognition of gender as a centrally important feature of child sexual abuse: the gender of the perpetrator rather than the victim. Whenever one argues the feminist position on child sexual abuse, the question is put: but don't women sexually abuse too?, as if the rare incidence of women abusing undermines the argument. Numbers are useful here.

All the research studies agree that the overwhelming majority of abusers are men. For example, in Russell's sample of 930 women, only ten cases of incestuous abuse by women were reported, despite a wide definition of abuse (Russell, 1986: 297). Few of the 'orthodox' experts choose to make this explicit. Although their statistics look at gender of 'victim', they rarely consider the gender of the 'perpetrator'. Instead, as happened in Cleveland, they talk about 'parents' or whether the abuse is within or outside the family. The report of the Mori poll is a good example of this; the tables distinguish between 'intrafamilial', 'extrafamilial' and 'stranger' abuse; the gender of the perpetrator is never mentioned (Baker and Duncan, 1985: 461).

Currently in the UK, many people are suggesting that the extent of sexual abuse by women is probably much greater than we think. The number of *cases* involving a female abuser has increased, but this is in the context of a rapid increase in the total number of cases. Feminists are often accused of being resistant to the idea that women may ever sexually abuse their children, but how much more resistant have the 'experts' been to the acceptance of sexual abuse as a predominantly male problem.

Women are quite capable of abusing power and trust, and of using children to fulfil their own emotional needs. They extremely rarely *sexually* abuse. To accept this is not to say that women never do, nor that women are morally superior. Simply, if we do not accept it, then we lose important clues to understanding *why* child sexual abuse occurs.

The increasing concern in the USA about the hidden incidence of sexual abuse by women led Russell and Finkelhor to carry out a detailed review of the research. Extraordinarily, they discovered that many of the early studies included women in the figures for perpetrators, not only when they had abused a child, but also when they had 'simply "allowed" sexual abuse to occur' (Russell, 1984: 219). Many of the cases of 'sexual abuse' by women were better described as inappropriate behaviour, such as overinvolvement with the child or continuing to sleep in the same bed, and were more likely to constitute emotional abuse. They found evidence that male abusers may be responsible for more serious and traumatic levels of sexual abuse than female abusers (Russell, 1984: 230).

They concluded from their review that 'the theory that perpetrators of sexual abuse are primarily men seems clearly supported' (Russell, 1984: 224). The most important question to come out of this research is one they themselves pose: 'So why are so many experts in the field currently arguing that the number of female perpetrators has been seriously underestimated?' (1984: 230).

The answer has to be because feminist theory is too threatening an opposition. Feminist theory, in taking account of gender in the examination of the phenomenon, does not exclude other inequalities. It must also take account of class and race and, crucially, the inequality and power relations associated with age. In most approaches to child sexual abuse, a great deal of attention is focused on 'the nature of childhood'. A number of 'childhoods' people the discussions. Some are very persistent: child as 'innocent'; child as 'seductress'; child as 'unliberated'; child as 'fantasizer'; child as 'home wrecker'; child as 'self-protector': all of these are roles set by adults for children to fill. But understanding the nature of childhood is not the key to understanding child sexual abuse.

Libertarianism: the legacy of Kinsey

This, we think, is the failure of the libertarian position: its apologists concentrate on proving a childhood sexuality, which is repressed and denied; thus, they say, a perfectly straightforward area of human sexuality is problematized. The libertarian arguments on 'adult-child sexual relations' were particularly important in the 1970s. They influenced the recommendations of the Criminal Law Revision Committee in 1976. They have enshrined in the discourse on child sexual abuse two

ideas that have proved remarkably difficult to shift and that continue to have a profound impact on intervention: it is intervention rather than abuse which causes trauma; and children can participate willingly in sexual activity with adults – indeed they desire it.

The recent history of these ideas, as they apply to child sexual abuse, can be said to begin with Kinsey:

> In many instances the law, in the course of punishing the offender, does more damage to more persons than was ever done by the individual in his illicit sexual activity. The child who has been raised in fear of all strangers and all physical manifestations of affection may ruin the lives of the married couple who had lived as useful and honorable citizens through half or more of a century, by giving her parents and the police a distorted version of the old man's attempt to bestow grandfatherly affection upon her. (Kinsey, 1953: 20).

Further:

> Some of the more experienced students of juvenile problems have come to believe that the emotional reactions of the parents, police officers, and other adults who discover that the child has had such a contact, may disturb the child more seriously than the sexual contacts themselves. (Kinsey, 1953: 121)

Throughout the 1970s, while the libertarian view was the predominant approach to child sexual abuse, women were beginning to voice their own experience and open the door to children's voices. At the same time important research studies (Finkelhor and Russell) were undertaken, influenced in their approach to interpreting their data by the women's movement campaigns on rape and domestic violence. Gradually the evidence was established which could challenge the liberal view, but it has persisted as an influence, and should be questioned.

The libertarian view is that there is nothing inherently harmful or problematic about adult–child sexual relations; it is the way childhood is constructed within a society that sets up a problem/panic where none need exist. If knowledge was available and guilt about sex abolished, children would not be traumatized by 'consensual sexual activity', would be empowered to say no to 'unwanted sexual contacts' and, presumably, since this is not explicit, sexual liberation would have stopped adults from wanting to have sex with unwilling children. The extreme form of the libertarian view is that of PIE (Paedophile Information Exchange), but libertarian arguments are adopted by some feminists. It is of course a Utopian argument, because it fails to take account of power relations between adults and children.

Libertarian politics have an honourable history as a force arguing for sexual freedoms: lesbian, homosexual and heterosexual, and it is not possible to argue that freedoms have not ensued. Equally convincing is the general argument about the repression of childhood sexuality and the repressive nature of the image of child as 'innocent'. What does not follow is that adult–child sexual relations are 'unproblematic'.

> One of the results of the sexual fix is the intense reluctance we have to
> envisage that there are real political-ethical problems in the area of
> sexual politics, that we really do need to develop a critical sexual politics.
> (Heath, 1982: 164)

As the forces of reaction gather, in a number of unholy alliances, it is crucial that just such a critical sexual politics is produced by feminists on this issue. We must not allow debate to be polarized as it is now: pleasure versus repression, family versus the state, decriminalization versus castration. The new initiatives produced by this confusion are very troubling. The whole movement to introduce so-called prevention programmes in schools is an excellent example of the inconsistencies, and the danger, of current government-supported practice. The support for 'educating children to say no' is happening at exactly the same time as the government is making ordinary sex education less and less possible; thus sex as danger becomes the constant message received by children; but children have been badly served by libertarian views.

The libertarian position on adult–child sexual relations was most emphatically put in a collection of essays called *Adult Sexual Interest in Children*, published in 1981, possibly as an intervention in the hounding of O'Carroll and PIE. In the summing up chapters by Plummer and West, the common erroneous assumptions are put. On children's experience of adult sexual attention: 'It is comparatively rare that the sex act is forced upon the child' (Plummer, 1981: 225). 'It is probable that most child "victims" could have removed themselves from the situation rather easily had they chosen to do so' (West 1981: 264).

Survivors' accounts differ startlingly: 'I would have had to kill him to stop him'; 'he said he did it because he loved me, all fathers did it' (Channel 4, 1984); 'I was so entirely frightened of him . . . he was the sort of person that you would have to do what he told' (quoted in Nelson, 1987: 42).

We know from women's accounts that a threat to kill their mother is often used. Research in the UK and USA bears out absolutely the range of threat, coercion, material and emotional bribery and blackmail used to enforce children's submission and ensure their silence. We also know that the power the adult has by virtue of his relationship to the child may be sufficient.

On the impact of adult sexual attention on children, Plummer and West have this to say: 'Although there is some evidence of the child experiencing short term shock the evidence for any long-term impact seems thin' (Plummer, 1981: 227). 'The effects of anxious probing by parents, followed by police interrogations, court proceedings and the imprisonment of someone to whom the child has been much attached, are certainly worse than the effects, if any, of the sexual activity itself' (West, 1981: 256). 'If sex by genuine consent were to be decriminalized, it would seem inconsistent to maintain incest as a crime, in the absence of force, coercion or abuse of parental authority' (West, 1981: 268). The evidence which most overwhelmingly dismisses these contentions is that of women and men survivors who have not had the experience of any state intervention, as well as the growing body of evidence on the connexion between child sexual abuse and severe mental health problems.

The most serious and considered recent expression of the libertarian position is in Jeffrey Weeks's book *Sexuality and its Discontents*. Weeks reports the strength of feminist arguments on the powerlessness of young people, particularly girls, in relation to adult men, and argues that young people are not fully aware of the sexual connotations of their actions. He also makes a distinction between children and adolescents. Yet he continues his argument by quoting heavily from the literature on paedophilia, which is biased towards stranger homosexual and heterosexual attacks on children, and especially quotes from O'Carroll's *Paedophilia: The Radical Case*. Thus he argues for adult sexual relations with young people on the basis of an argument that children are sexual beings, that the trauma involved in intervention is greater than the trauma of the act itself, and that the paedophile has been given a bad name, being chiefly, in reality, distinguished by 'an intense, but often highly affectionate and even excessively sentimental regard for young people' (Weeks, 1985: 227).

This line of argument has a number of disturbing features. First it uses a particular language of euphemism to persuade: adult–child sexual relations are described as inter- or cross-generational, by which is not meant sex between thirty-year-olds and sixty-year-olds. Secondly this *particular* view of childhood sexuality derives from a particular Eurocentric history of childhood which takes no account of the gender differences which existed, and seems to assume a lost golden age of childhood sexuality drawn from Aries' examples of the childhood of Louis XIII (O'Carroll, 1980; Langfeldt, 1981). A cursory reading of Aries' description of the childhood of Louis XIII reveals a childhood sexuality no less socially constructed and no less a product of adult definition than now.

Incongruously in Weeks's work, which has contributed so much to the notion of a socially constructed sexuality, it appears to incorporate an essentialist view of sexuality as a biological force requiring particular expression; thus paedophilia is entirely taken for granted. We are offered no deconstruction of paedophilia.

Though women have benefitted from sexual liberation arguments, they are 'male' arguments. They have no politics of relationships, and women just do not feature. Of course women and children are sexual beings, but this is no argument for the acceptability of any male desires.

Finally, we come to consent, the subject of much debate within the libertarian approach, and for centuries an issue within sexual politics. In our view there is no debate about whether children can consent to sexual relations with adults. To be meaningful, consent must be freely given on the basis of knowledge, understanding and equality of relationship. We cannot conceive of a situation where children and adolescents could be deemed to have such knowledge and understanding. Apart from the risks associated with sexual activity – pregnancy, VD, AIDS, cervical cancer, risks which adults have to attend to with forethought and planning – sex in this society is, as Weeks says, heavily burdened with meanings and consequences hard enough for experienced, 'liberated' adults to understand.

This position does not rule out a childhood sexuality, nor an adolescent one. No one should argue against changing the ways in which people speak to children about sexuality, nor against openness about children's own sexuality; and we should strongly oppose the government's policies on sex education. There is, however, no evidence of a simple relationship between children's knowledge and understanding of sex, and protection from abuse (Nash and West, 1985: 76). An age of consent must be maintained, below which consent has to be deemed ungiveable. Whichever age the boundary is, it will be an imposition on some young people and an inadequate protection for others. How much of an imposition it is to adult men is a complete irrelevance.

Psychoanalysis: the legacy of Freud

Psychoanalysis also has things to say about child sexual abuse, but especially incestuous abuse. It is extremely difficult to do justice to the many aspects of incest which psychoanalysis addresses, and some of these are explored elsewhere in this volume. We therefore propose to do no more than briefly survey psychoanalytic ideas, their currency and their influence on practice.

Though psychoanalysis is not the dominant theory on child sexual abuse, it is powerful in the influence it has had, and continues to have,

on the way that incest is thought and talked of, and the impact it has had on all casework and therapeutic practice.

Freud's influence on the meaning of 'incest' is profound. He clearly found 'incest' a deeply apt metaphor for the transformation of animal into civilized 'man'. His description of the sexual as the instinctive force which requires restraint, control and channeling to allow the existence of a stable social order continues to appeal to the collective imagination. He saw the incest taboo as the primary restraint, and he found in Greek myth a fruitful source. In Sophocles' *Oedipus the King*, Jocasta says: 'Nor need this mother-marrying frighten you; many a man has dreamt as much' (Sophocles, 1947: 52).

In Sophocles' play and Freud's incestuous world, incest is mother–son (the least common); the 'Father' is absent as a character, being present as the punishing superego, the holder of the Law. It is a truly patriarchal imaginary world, the 'goddess' nowhere to be seen; but Freud was a man of his time, and we should not berate him for being so. The furious debates about whether Freud or psychoanalysis recognized the existence of widespread sexual abuse of children are to some extent irrelevant. Exculpatory myths and denial are produced in avoidance of painful realities: that the law-givers have feet of clay. What was important in constructing the mythology of incest (seductive children asking for it, and children making it up) were the conjunction of particular psychoanalytic ideas with a particular time and place, and a long extant discourse about children, men, women, sexuality and incest.

The collective anxiety, panic and confusion set off by discussion of child sexual abuse can be seen as the unsurprising response to the challenging of a founding idea of our civilization: that incest is the boundary between stability and chaos. If, as the supposed facts show, incest is rife everywhere, then chaos is foreclosing on us.

Psychoanalysis, in supporting this meaning for incest, has assisted in the denial of actual abuse; but it should not be accused of minimizing the trauma of incest. Indeed, quite the reverse. Anna Freud has argued that:

> Far from existing as a phantasy, incest is thus also a fact, more widespread among the population in certain periods than in others. Where the chances of harming a child's normal development growth are concerned, it ranks higher than abandonment, neglect, physical maltreatment or any other form of abuse. It would be a fatal mistake to underestimate either the importance or the frequency of its actual occurrence. (Freud, 1981: 34)

Winnicott says that seduction brought children 'to a real, instead of an imaginary, sexual life, and spoiled the child's perquisite: unlimited play' (Winnicott, 1961: 109).

Psychoanalysis, then, has a great deal to say about the meaning of the event to the individual child or adult, and much of this is acute, sensitive and complex. Only the literature of women survivors can better communicate the terrible confusion that a sexually abused child feels:

> Could I tell her [mother] now? The terrible pain assured me that I couldn't. What he did to me, and what I allowed, must have been very bad if already God let me hurt so much. (Angelou, 1984: 79)

The major contribution psychoanalysis makes to theory and practice on child sexual abuse is the understanding of this ambivalence, the support that it gives sufferers in the confusion of their feelings, and the discipline that enables its practitioners to hear the unspeakable and thus allow it to be said. In having a place for childhood sexuality, for fantasy, and a 'morality' for parents and adults (which is often crushing in its demands), it has a way of theorizing the internalization of guilt which abused children and adults feel. It is a common experience that children feel love as well as hatred or fear for their abuser. Sometimes, sadly, they say that the abuser was the only person in their lives who gave them any attention or affection. This is then sometimes interpreted to mean that the girl's *real* feeling was to welcome the abuse, or that it wasn't really harmful. Or there is an attempt to weigh up which of the two feelings is the stronger. What psychoanalysis enables us to understand is that both feelings can exist simultaneously.

There are, however, difficulties in the traditional therapeutic method in helping recovery:

> The greatest difficulties come when there has been a seduction in the patient's childhood, in which case there must be experienced in the course of treatment a delusion that the therapist is repeating the seduction. (Winnicott, 1961: 86).

The vehicle of transference within the therapeutic process, and the emphasis on the patient being responsible for the journey to insight and meaning, may provide overwhelming stumbling blocks to a sufferer's capacity to use psychotherapy. In order to achieve a meaning other than self-blame or self-hatred, the 'rewriting' of a survivor's history may require, if it is to start, the relocation of the patient in a different landscape. This is something that women know well; consciousness-raising is perhaps the most effective way of beginning the challenge to an internalized ideology.

In theorizing about child sexual abuse, psychoanalysis is within a patriarchal ideology. Where this is most evident is in what psychoanalysis has to say about abusers. The abuser's progress to abuse is generally understood as the man's response to a childhood history, featuring acute anxiety about sexual adequacy, fear of castration and rage at the 'mother'. This of course individualizes the problem and takes for granted a particular construction of male–female relationships and masculine sexuality. It asks no questions about this association of powerlessness, violence and sexuality in male sexuality and none about the 'mother', and thus abandons men and abusers to a theory and practice that offer little hope of rescue from the idea of uncontrollable male sexuality and misogyny.

The orthodoxy: family dysfunction

Though libertarian and psychoanalytic ideas have a place in constructing the current discourse on child sexual abuse, the discourse is dominated by another approach. It focuses on the 'family' in which abuse occurs, not in order to expose problematic sexual politics, but in order to enshrine 'normal' family relationships. The approach is not presented as a 'theory' supported by evidence, or as an interpretation of a set of 'facts', but instead is put forward as an orthodoxy, as the *truth*, by a particularly influential, mainly male, group of professionals in Britain.

No debates are ever posed, nor any public discussion of these ideas offered. They are associated with various 'institutions', such as Great Ormond Street Hospital for Sick Children, the Tavistock Clinic, the National Society for the Prevention of Cruelty to Children (NSPCC) and the National Children's Bureau, and are embodied within the DHSS guidelines on how to intervene in cases of child sexual abuse. These professionals are the accepted authorities in the field, and they advise the DHSS and the Home Office. Their power and status in this area means that they are difficult to challenge, and their ideas are couched in technical language which serves to mystify people and to hide what is actually being said. The approach is chilling in its incorporation of the most reactionary sexual politics into an apparently reasoned, reasonable and caring theory and practice.

Until recently, there has been a complete split between the work and ideas of Rape Crisis, Women's Aid and Incest Survivors on the one hand, and the orthodox approach on the other. Individual feminists working in the statutory agencies have been isolated. The presentation of feminist ideas on theory and practice at conferences and in articles has been a revelation and almost a liberation to many professional workers, who have been troubled by the orthodoxy and relieved to discover that there is an alternative way of working. The orthodox approach is seductive in its certainty. People faced with child sexual abuse desperately desire certainty about what to do and what to say.

The approach derives from 'systems theory', which has been increasingly influential in social work and family psychiatry. It has been adapted from electronics and applied to the study of families and groups, and is the theory underlying 'family therapy'. What is crucial for our purposes is that the focus of concern is the *family*, rather than particular individuals who may have abused or been abused. Indeed, they frequently refer to 'sexually abused families' (NSPCC, 1984: 14). Simply, it describes families as 'systems' which organize themselves so as to maintain a 'homeostatic' or 'steady state'. This is achieved by each part of the system influencing and being influenced by other parts. Interaction is governed by rules which are usually observed from outside by a trained therapist/observer, but which are not agreed explicitly by the family members. 'Family dysfunction' is a particular brand of systems theory, unsophisticated in its conception of family members' roles, and of power relations, which are completely unquestioned.

The presentation of this approach usually starts with an acknowledgement that child sexual abuse is far more common than professionals had accepted until recently. The idea that children either lie or fantasize about sexual abuse is explicitly rejected, and it is categorically stated that the child is not to blame, that the abuser is wholly responsible. However, the explanation which follows takes account neither of how common child sexual abuse is, nor of the majority of child sexual abuse which is not father–child incest, nor of how a 'family dysfunction' explanation draws responsibility away from the abuser. The approach does not even follow through the logic of its position.

The family, then, is seen as a system with two levels of functioning: a 'surface action' of the roles and relationships which can be observed in the family, and a 'depth structure' of underlying needs and emotions. In a normal, healthy or 'functional' family, the 'depth' needs for care, warmth and sex are satisfied through the surface action of the family, and traditional gender and age roles are an important way of achieving this. In a 'dysfunctional' family, however, the surface action of the family does not satisfy the underlying needs of the family members. There are various 'remedies' or 'solutions' to this dysfunction, one of which may be a 'sexualization of what should be nurturant physical contact' (Mrazek and Bentovim, 1981: 168). Thus sexual abuse is a *symptom* of what is wrong in the family, or even a 'solution' to the dysfunction. It is argued that there are 'many different routes' (Mrazek and Bentovim, 1981: 168) to this incestuous family surface action, and other workers have distinguished between different sorts of sexually abusive families. In all cases the problem is not the sexual abuse, but the underlying dysfunction. Once the family system is analysed in detail to see why it has broken down, then in almost every case it is the mother who is seen as ultimately responsible. There is an unwritten assumption that families are functional when men's needs are met.

The textbook of this approach is *Child Sexual Abuse Within the Family*, published in 1984. In it, Furniss distinguishes between 'conflict avoiding' and 'conflict regulating' families (Porter, 1984: 11), in which the sexual abuse serves the function either of avoiding conflict between the parents, or of helping to regulate it. He argues that: 'Two different patterns of maternal behaviour occur in the two different types of family' (Porter, 1984: 12). In the 'conflict avoiding families' it seems that the mother 'sets the rules for emotional relationships and for the way sexual and emotional matters are talked about' (Porter, 1984: 12). She is emotionally distant from the daughter(s) who are being abused, although she may compensate for this by compulsive caretaking. If the child tells her mother about the abuse it will be denied or dismissed.

By contrast, in the 'conflict regulating family', 'the mother is deficient in practical as well as emotional support for the children. She becomes their "pseudo-equal"' (Porter, 1984: 12). In this kind of family it is said that the girl who is being abused may have adopted the role of mother. Conflict, and even violence, between the parents is overt, and 'the child is "sacrificed" to regulate this conflict and avoid family breakdown' (Porter, 1984: 12). In all this there is no discussion of the father or his role, except to suggest that in the 'conflict avoiding' family, the 'non-spoken collusion increases the father's emotional dependence on the mother and keeps him firmly bound to the family' (Porter, 1984: 13): mother is ultimately responsible again.

Elsewhere, in the same book, there is a discussion about whether some children are more vulnerable to abuse than others. There is a suggestion that children denied affection are at risk. In addition:

A child is at risk when a mother is over-punitive over sexual matters; not close or affectionate with the child; often ill or absent – rejecting or

rejected by her family; poorly educated; socially isolated or with few
friends . . .; depressed, psychotic, or dependent on drugs; and most
importantly, sexually abused in her own childhood. (Porter, 1984: 8)

The father's behaviour is discussed only as a response to the mother's
rejection or withdrawal, which may lead to the father and children
turning to each other

for support, practical assistance, or comfort and the foundations of an
incestuous relationship are laid. In other cases a man deprived of his
conjugal rights may turn to the nearest available source of gratification –
a dependent child. (Porter, 1984: 9)

Furthermore, there is no attempt to explain why it is *men* rather
than women who sexually abuse their children. So male sexuality is
seen as driven and uncontrollable: 'These men may misunderstand the
adolescent's behaviour and be sexually aroused by it; or physical
chastisement may lead the perpetrator to the excitement that blends
into sexual activity' (Porter, 1984: 9). Poor men! It is up to women not
only to nurture and care for their men adequately, and to control their
own desires, but also to control men's sexuality. Since men are not able
to control themselves, and are seen as being 'addicted', there is always
the danger that it will happen again. Bentovim and others argue that
children are safe within the family only if their mothers can protect
them.

In all these accounts women are described as actively withdrawing,
being punitive or depriving men of their conjugal rights, while men are
described as if they were children, more frequently passive, aroused by
what others do to them, or spontaneously acting and in need of control.
Thus Bentovim speaks of a man 'finding himself' touching the genitals
of a five-year-old, just as we might 'find ourselves' assaulting a
policeman or robbing a bank.

While the approach concentrates on abuse within the family and in
particular by fathers, it is suggested that families in which children are
neglected or not valued as individuals may also fail to protect their
children from abuse from the wider family, friends and even strangers.
At the same time, and without picking up the contradictions, it is argued
that responsibility and blame should be removed entirely from individuals and placed on the family system: everyone's a victim of the
family breakdown. This removal of blame is followed by a plea for
rejection of a punitive model and its replacement with a therapeutic one,
since 'the emphasis on punishing the perpetrators which was prevalent
in the English approach and in the media meant that victims would
conceal the problem and make it harder to identify' (Bentovim, quoted in
the *Guardian*, 8. 9. 87).

There are feminists who are family therapists (Bograd, 1984; Pilais
and Anderton, 1986). They suggest that feminism and family therapy
need not be incompatible, but they distinguish between the *explanation*

given for the abuse happening and the therapeutic methods adopted. Family therapy may provide a useful way of helping a secret in the family to be disclosed. The incestuous assault could be described as the cause, rather than the symptom, of family dysfunction. These refinements have not yet reached Great Ormond Street.

Subcultures and cycles
The family dysfunction approach often incorporates other popular views, which need to be questioned: the 'cultural theory' and the 'cycle of abuse'. Thus it is often suggested, despite no evidence, that 'there are isolated communities or subcultures in which incest is accepted readily' (Kempe and Kempe, 1984: 51), or that incest is more likely in cultures which do not conform to traditional sex roles. These ideas feed racist myths about 'pathological' Black families and class stereotypes about so-called 'chaotic' or 'disorganized' working-class families. Many abusers tell children that abuse is quite normal in their family/culture: they are 'good cultural theorists' (Nelson, 1987: 48).

The other notion, the 'cycle of abuse' is taken as a 'fact': men abuse because they were abused in childhood; women who were abused in childhood do not themselves abuse, but they marry abusers and become 'colluding' mothers. These ideas are not based on sound research, but are derived from the experience of clinicians. No one has investigated either the number of men who were abused in childhood who do not go on to abuse their children, or the women survivors who do not marry abusers. Given the frequency of child sexual abuse, any relationship that does exist between mothers who were abused in childhood and abused daughters may well arise by chance. Indeed, if all men who abuse their daughters had been abused themselves, it would mean a disproportionately huge amount of undisclosed abuse of boys. Finally, there has been no attempt to describe a causal link between childhood abuse and adult abusing or collusion.

It is important not to underestimate the power of these ideas. Not only do they have a spurious liberal appeal, by saying that individual men are not to blame, but they are also internalized by many women. Their effect is to absolve the abuser of responsibility (he's a victim of his

own childhood) and to add to the abuse done to women by claiming that their abuse in childhood is largely to blame for their own children being abused.

Mother blaming

The extent of mother blaming in the family dysfunction approach is quite breathtaking:

> Incest . . . is not initiated by the child but by the adult male, with the mother's complicity. Stories from mothers that they 'could not be more surprised' can generally be discounted – we have simply not seen an innocent mother in long-standing incest, although the mother escapes the punishment that her husband is likely to suffer.
>
> Why do mothers play such an important role in facilitating incest between father and daughter? Often a very dependent mother is frantic to hold on to her man for her own needs and the financial support he provides, and sees the daughter as a way of providing a younger, more attractive sexual bond within the family than she can offer. This is especially true if she is frigid, rejected sexually, or herself promiscuous. (Kempe and Kempe, 1978: 66)

We want to expose in some detail the mother blaming in the professional literature, before suggesting an alternative way of understanding the ways that women respond to the sexual abuse of their children. For it is the view of 'mothers', and the implication of this view for practice, that most clearly divides the 'family dysfunction' and feminist positions. Earlier we unpicked the theory and demonstrated that, in this approach, families are dysfunctional when 'mothers' are not adequately performing their role. This criticism has been made before and often. Yet as Sarah Nelson says:

> Where incest is concerned, many assumptions are being swept away by the tide. Yet professionals cling to the collusive wife theory like drowning men grasping at flotsam. Could it be because it is such a powerful defence against admitting the male abuse of power? And because without it family therapists might be like emperors without clothes? These are harsh questions which they owe it to their own integrity to ask. (Nelson, 1987: 108)

On the surface it appears that some feminist ideas have had an influence on professionals, but scratch it, and we are back to the mothers again. For example, in a recent paper, Baker and Duncan, working within a model of family dysfunction, both acknowledge that it is *men* who sexually abuse and *appear* to have taken on board some feminist arguments. Thus they argue that in order to understand why it is men who sexually abuse children we have to look at the way men are socialized to separate sex from affection, and to be aroused by people smaller and less powerful than themselves. They go on to argue that 'men are not helpless victims of their own uncontrollable sexual urges' (Baker and Duncan, 1986: 262) and that most men, even if they have fantasies about children, will not act on them. However, they suggest that some men will overcome their internal inhibitions, because they themselves were abused in childhood (cycle of abuse), or because of their social or material situation (poverty, unemployment). In these cases the men require 'external constraints', and again one person in the family is ultimately responsible for these!

> In families where the mother is absent, sick or powerless or spends large amounts of time away while others, including the father, care for the children there is an increased opportunity for abuse to take place. The father whose self-esteem has been damaged by redundancy or unemployment may have ample opportunity to reassert himself by abusing a child as he is cast into the role of primary caretaker.
> (Baker and Duncan, 1986: 263).

It is interesting to note in passing that if 'opportunity' were an important factor then one might expect a very high level of abuse from women.

So, starting from some ideas that we might have sympathy with, we have been taken on a tour of several theories and ended right back in the same place, with the ideas of uncontrollable male urges, female responsibility to control men, the collusive wife, and the absent, withdrawn or rejecting mother. It is these ideas that are the most dangerous and damaging parts of the current orthodoxy.

It is encouraging to find that some workers within the 'family dysfunction' framework are finding that the practice does not always bear out the theory. Thus, an account of 'Group Work with Mothers Whose Children Have Been Sexually Abused', carried out at Great Ormond Street, states:

> In our experience it is unwise to assume that all mothers contribute to or condone the abuse. Indeed it may be that less weight should be given to psychological explanations of mothers' roles in child sexual abuse and more to factors which lead to them perceiving themselves as powerless to alter their own or their children's situation (Hildebrand and Forbes, 1987: 288)

What is not recognized in the theory of the 'collusive' mother is that we have all absorbed the ideology of motherhood: mothers are supposed to care for and protect us; we blame them when things go wrong; often they are the only safe recipient of children's anger. If children are being sexually abused, then it is assumed that their mothers *should* somehow know it and stop it. Child and adult survivors' anger at their mother, and their belief that she must have known, is taken as evidence that she did in fact know, but practitioners must not assume this. They would easily perceive the distinction between feelings and reality in another context, for instance bereavement.

Some mothers do refuse to believe that sexual abuse has occurred, or know and do nothing, or are angry with and blame their daughter, or feel that they are themselves to blame. This is taken as evidence of collusion. Yet we know that denial, anger and guilt are common responses to loss. This kind of event, especially if it occurs within the family, is a tragic loss for everyone. The woman has lost her view of herself as 'wife' and mother. She has lost the fantasy family; her family and her relationships with other family members will never be the same again. The desperate desire of many mothers is: 'let it not have happened, let it not be true'. Jan Macleod and Patricia Bell of Glasgow Women's Support Project sum it up beautifully:

> A woman does not commit her life and security to a man she believes capable of molesting his own children. Psychiatrists and experts in this field cannot find any 'identifying' features among abusers – so how are women supposed to identify an abuser before they marry him? People will very readily talk about 'colluding mothers' but we should ask ourselves: if you were told, or began to suspect, that your brother or husband or friend was abusing his children, would you go straight to the police? In [their] powerless position women are expected to be more aware, more resourceful and more courageous than the doctors, teachers, social workers etc, who make up a society which through denial colludes with child abuse. Professional workers often condemn 'colluding mothers' in one breath, and in the next say 'I'm sure that there is incest in such and such a family, but I don't know what to do about it.' (Quoted in Nelson, 1987: 70)

In criticizing the idea of 'mother collusion', we also have to be careful not to put in its place our own idealization of mothers. We should not insist that mothers are always perfect; we know they aren't, and why should they be? Many women *do* believe their daughters, *do* protect them, *do* act in their best interests, and have always done so (Clark, 1987: 101), but a feminist analysis also explains why some women may be unable to protect their children, and why the failure to do so 'is regarded as particularly loathsome' (Wattenberg, 1985: 203).

It is not possible to overestimate either the power of 'mother collusion' ideas on lay people, on mothers and on abused children themselves or their enormous influence on practice. Practitioners will engage in lengthy discussions at case conferences on the mother's role. Some will see all mothers as collusive; others will look at the mother's response to the information that her child has been abused, interpreting anger and denial as evidence of 'collusion'. From this will come decisions about appropriate measures for child protection and therapeutic plans. In protection work, children are seen as equally unsafe with their mother as with the abuser, and are received into care, as appears to have happened in Cleveland. Therapy starts from an assumption of mother's collusion and pursues this through family meetings and individual work. This leads to a belief that the 'best' outcome for a woman who has been abused is that she understand and forgive her father and recognize her mother's responsibility, in the context of a 'rehabilitated' family system (Baillie, 1983; Owen, 1987).

A collusion *is* at work here: a collusion with a set of assumptions which allows families to remain exactly as they are, and which can have a ruinous effect on children and families. 'Clearly the attitude of the therapist toward the mother is pivotal. The therapist's unstated pursuit of evidence for the therapist's *assumption* of the mother's collusion will threaten the entire therapeutic process' (Wattenberg, 1985: 209). It can also drive a wedge between mother and daughter, widening difference and exacerbating distress. For many survivors, part of their anger with their father is that he denied them the possibility of a good relationship with their mother; therapy ought not to collude with this.

While it is true that women's and children's interests are not identical, it is also true that if workers attempt to build an alliance between mother and daughter at the time of disclosure, both do benefit emotionally: the child in feeling less rejected, less alone; the mother in feeling less guilty, less detached.

If we adopt a feminist perspective we will not automatically condemn a mother as 'collusive' if she does not want to believe what has happened, or even if we discover that she did know and did nothing. We will concentrate on giving care and attention to women, recognizing the difficulties of their position, the complexities of their feelings, the meaning for them of what has happened.

The feminist challenge

And so, to feminism, and its challenge to the orthodoxy. Feminist theory starts with gender. In looking at why children get sexually abused we are not looking at some 'Neanderthal' drive, nor at problem families, but at problematic sexual and adult–child politics.

If we look at the history of child sexual abuse as an issue, we find that it was not discovered by sociologists, psychiatrists, social workers or journalists. Like rape and domestic violence, child sexual abuse was brought to public attention by women, particularly women survivors. The voices of women survivors and workers in Women's Aid, Rape Crisis and Incest Survivors' groups have told child sexual abuse as a different story. It is an overwhelmingly convincing story. It says: don't tell us we like it, we want it, we need it or we agree to it. Don't tell us you're freeing us from sexual repression, educating us for a more fulfilling adult life. Don't tell us you do this because you love us, don't tell us you do this because nobody loves you. Don't tell us we are dirty. Don't tell us we are worthless. And don't tell us we can't recover. You may have fucked our bodies, but you're not going to fuck our minds.

The process of recovery, of moving from victim to survivor, has a central phase of anger. The process of developing a feminist theory mirrors this. There is plenty of scope for rage in reading the annals of academic inquiry into child sexual abuse; but if we are to move from conspiracy theory to a revolutionary one, we have to move from anger to analysis.

The elaboration of a feminist analysis of child sexual abuse began with Florence Rush's book, *The Best Kept Secret*, published in 1980. Herman (1981) in the USA and Nelson (1982) in the UK have developed the arguments, which are borne out by the research on child sexual abuse undertaken by feminists and others, and by the autobiographical and fictional accounts of incestuous abuse.

Adults, women and men; adolescents, boys and girls, have the means to abuse (age, power, status, love) and they have or can easily arrange the opportunity within the family; but only men (and a very few women) have the motive, the desire. Though both men and women abuse power over children by engaging in physical or emotional abuse, it is men who abuse children sexually. Child sexual abuse is, then, one part of a spectrum of male violence against women and children. Instead of asking why it is that we problematize children's sexuality, feminists ask why is it that men wish to objectify children's sexuality. Why is it that male rage is turned on women and children? Helped by analyses of the ideology of racism, feminists look for answers to the history and the cultural representation of masculinity, femininity and sexuality. For the objectifying of others' sexuality is not a biologically determined masculine characteristic; women can and do arrive there too. Finding the representations is only too easy. From the rape of the Sabine women, a potent artistic image for generations of painters, rape, personal power and state power have been linked. Rome, says the history, was established on rape: the founding of a dynastic, imperial state depending on the male as sexual aggressor.

The long history of misogyny in western Europe has its current expression everywhere from violent and degrading pornography to respectable films and novels, from working-class pubs to Oxbridge colleges. The long-established discourse on male sexuality as subject and everything else as object dominates cultural expression. The association of masculinity with domination, of sexual dominance with personal 'success', is all pervasive.

In western culture, there has for 500 years also been an association of sexual domination and racism:

> I want to suggest to you that rape bears a direct relationship to all of the existing power structures in a given society. This relationship is not a simple mechanical one, but rather involves complex structures reflecting the complex interconnectedness of race, gender, and class oppression which characterizes that society. If we do not attempt to understand the nature of sexual violence as it relates to racial, class and governmental violence and power, we cannot even begin to develop strategies which will allow us to eventually purge our society of the oppressiveness of rape. (Davis, 1985: 9)

This is the ideology that not only makes possible sexual violence of every kind, but also renders it invisible. It is only the latter part of the ideology, the invisibility, that is currently threatened. It is a mistake to separate off any particular manifestation of the spectrum of violence and to see it as a special case. Simply, these politics, that history, this culture ensure that some men will be able to abuse their own daughters.

The impact of the ideology on the collective and individual male internal world is also easy to narrate. Generally boys and men learn to experience their sexuality as an overwhelming and uncontrollable force; they learn to focus their sexual feelings on submissive objects, and they learn the assertion of their sexual desires, the expectation of having them serviced. Obviously this is a crude account of a complex phenomenon; male sexuality is not one-dimensional, and within a culture oppositional ideologies exist (for example, men as caretakers of their families, gentle lovers and protectors of their daughters), and have their impact on self-definition and cultural practices. Thus all men do not abuse, and sexual violence against women and children will have a different meaning, and different prevalences, within different societies at different times.

Even if the demand of the ideology on male self-esteem is high (as many argue), and the resulting anxieties and inadequacy crushing, then all men do not escape from inadequacy and anxiety into sexual violence. For some men, an escape may be managed and reinforced through fantasy and pornography. But those who do abuse seem to find this conjunction of sexual pleasure and domination so heady a mixture that they feel constantly driven to repeat it. Some say they are tormented by remorse or self-disgust and want to be stopped. Beyond this we know very little about the men who abuse, or why they do. What is clear is that there is no help to be got in answering this from studying their children, their 'victims', their mothers, wives or girlfriends.

Some men are turning their attention to the 'problem of masculinity'.

Some theorists . . . draw attention to differential patterns of conscious and unconscious socialization for boys and girls which, together with wider social images of masculine sexuality, have the effect of constructing men as alienated from intimate relations and from our sexuality . . . The characteristic patterns of masculinity, focusing on independence and 'hardness' and turning away from intimacy and nurture, follow from this. In particular it produces a severely narrowed rendering of sexuality, operating primarily in two convergent ways. First, sex is one of the few means by which men aspire to closeness with others, and as such it becomes the carrier of all the unexpressed desires that men's emotional illiteracy produces. However this same process makes sex dangerous to men whose identity is built on the denial of emotion; sex then becomes split off, limited to the activity of the penis, an act rather than an encounter. At the same time, sex becomes tied up with competition, separation and power – something used to bolster a man's sense of masculinity rather than to create a bond with another. The link between such a form of masculinity and sexual abuse is apparent: it is not just present, but *inherent* in a mode of personality organization that rejects intimacy. Sex as defence and as triumph slides naturally into sex as rejection and degradation of the other. . . .

This is not, of course, to say that all men actually abuse children, nor that there are no differences between those that do and those that do not . . . There are also important and difficult questions concerning the processes whereby most men learn *not* to abuse children – processes presumably connected with the quality of their relationships in early life, internalization of moral constraints, and the development of capacities to form positive sexual and emotional relationships with adults. But if there are systematic factors that make men more likely to sexually abuse children, then these factors will be present more or less strongly in all men. (Frosh, 1987: 335)

Frosh explains sex as defence, triumph, rejection and degradation, but not sex as rage. He sees the embargo on emotional expression as on affection, softness, tenderness, sadness; he does not mention anger and rage. It seems to us that men get every encouragement to express anger. If emotion is sexualized this explains why men sexually abuse and perceive it as non-abusive; it does not explain the sexualization of rage and anger, unless what is suggested is an inability to separate tenderness and brutality. If this is so, then instead of seeing the source of sexual violence in rage at the mother, perhaps it should be seen as rage at men, at the father, at the self, that is displaced onto and acted out against women and children, and instead of perceiving other men as threatening, which is terrifying and unacceptable, the threat is perceived in women where it can be controlled.

The wilderness of the playground, where boys learn so much about domination, submission and the basics of misogyny – the worthlessness of girls – may have a lot to say about 'those who do and those who don't'. Certainly the figure, pathetic in the face of authority and brutish at

home, which peoples the clinical accounts, bears a striking resemblance to the school bully, ingratiating and terrifying by turn.

Whatever difficulties exist in childhood, family, relationship, work and lifestyle, whatever freedom or repression exists about child and adult sexuality, it is a particular construction of masculinity that enables men to sexually abuse children. A feminist analysis places at the centre of an explanation of child sexual abuse the 'problem of masculinity'. It attempts to stop the collusion of theory with sexual politics, to make sexual violence visible, and to construct a different meaning for it. This is not simply academic. From a different meaning arises a different practice.

From theory to practice

Feminist critiques of the orthodox approach draw out the woman, mother, and child blaming, and the essentialist view of male sexuality that it incorporates, be it ever so apparently scientifically and academically respectable. The first aim of feminist practice is to attack this and to argue an alternative theory. This is already underway: witness the accounts of feminist practice included in this volume, and the burgeoning feminist literature on child sexual abuse.

The next step is influencing policy at all levels, and this too is well underway: for example, the moves to enable the exclusion of abusive men so that children can stay in the non-abusive parts of their family, as outlined in the Islington policy and guidelines and recent discussion at the Labour Party conference. There have been changes in police practice, and the government proposes changes in the rules of evidence. Some feminists fear the gifts of a Tory establishment, wondering whether other less acceptable outcomes are the real motive behind the change.

What should a feminist policy and practice look like? Is such a thing possible within a statutory agency? If our analysis of child sexual abuse leads to the conclusion that it is a product of the construction of male sexuality within a particular form of society, then how can single state agencies, let alone individual workers, do anything more than alleviate the consequences of such abuse?

There have tended to be two feminist responses to this dilemma; either feminists should remain outside the statutory sector, and continue to offer women and children an alternative service through Rape Crisis, Women's Aid, and Incest Survivors' groups, or feminist social workers should see their work as part of the process of overthrowing the capitalist patriarchal state (Dominelli, 1986). Recently, however, a more complex analysis of state intervention has brought the work and ideas of feminists and some statutory agencies closer together.

It is not surprising that the issue of child sexual abuse should expose the inadequacies of the left's position on state intervention. The left has generally seen social work as the instrument of state control of working-class families. The use women and children have made of voluntary and statutory social work agencies to redress some of the imbalance of power within the family has long been invisible, and only recently written about (Gordon, 1985). It has been possible in looking at the physical abuse of children to argue a relationship between poverty and stress and abuse (Parton, 1985). No such relationship exists for child sexual abuse: sexual politics have to be taken into acount. We cannot continue to see the family as a monolithic structure serving everyone's needs. We have to admit the inequalities of power and the conflicts of interest that exist within families. The 'traditional' left is no less threatened by a feminist critique of the family in its male hegemony than the right, as recent crudely argued pieces in the *News on Sunday* (2 May 1987) and the *Socialist Worker* (22 August 1987) show. This is not to argue for no debates about intervention: only for a more complex appreciation of the issues.

Intervention and racism

There never has been a 'golden age' of no intervention in people's lives. Constraints and controls on how people 'parent' have always been exercised by communities, though of course the form of these has been historically specific, and has incorporated the dominant ideology on 'good parenting'. This leads to a heavy class and racist bias in the practice of intervention, the imposition of white middle-class heterosexual norms of good parenting on people and the assumption that poor single parents, Black parents or lesbian parents need 'improving'. Inequalities in child care are just that – the result of unequal resources – but there is nothing wrong, racist or anti-working class in saying that certain behaviours toward children are unacceptable. It is possible for workers to make judgements in groups other than their own, though an understanding of racism and different cultural patterns is essential if accurate conclusions about the meaning of interactions are to be made. The problem comes in acting on a judgement.

In a racist society, it is extremely important to be aware of the injustice into which a Black family may be delivered in invoking criminal proceedings, in taking children into care and in separating children and families. If the family has a central place in people's identity, how much more so for Black people for whom it may be one of the few places of retreat from racism. It is also necessary to recognize the impact that racism can have on the meaning of the event. A Black child

who has internalized racism may equate being Black with being bad, and the guilt that all abused children experience may confirm those feelings. She may also find it harder to 'tell', since it may feel like an even greater betrayal of her family than it is to a white child.

We cannot, however, simply be anti-interventionist, thinking we are being progressive, because this does mean closing our eyes to the abuse of children in families; but we do have to take cognizance of the implications of state intervention. Feminists have a lot to say on this.

Feminist practice

Feminist practice has been born from the initiatives of the women's movement on rape and domestic violence. The growth of awareness of child sexual abuse started from hearing women talk about childhood abuse, from women asking for help to protect their children, and from girls and young women ringing the crisis lines because of abuse. These groups have built up a formidable body of knowledge and experience, from working with women and children who have been assaulted, on what their feelings may be, on the process of recovery, and on what is helpful. This expertise should be acknowledged, and the knowledge used to improve practice elsewhere. (See articles from the Brixton Black Women's Centre, Glasgow Women's Support Project and the Norwich Consultants on Sexual Violence in this volume, and London Rape Crisis Centre, 1984.)

However, these women's resources are not adequate to protect children, because they do not have statutory power; and the principles underlying their practice – that women have the right to complete control over what action is taken following an assault – cannot be straightforwardly extended to children, though ChildLine appears to be doing so. Statutory services are essential, but they must be organized to empower not oppress women and children.

Feminist social workers, often isolated in their work, have begun to organize specifically around child sexual abuse. The power and potential of this is demonstrated by the development of the Islington policy and guidelines. A conference held in April 1987, 'Child Sexual Abuse: Towards a Feminist Professional Practice', attracted a large number of women working within a wide range of voluntary and statutory agencies. The interchange of ideas and experience was exciting, and it has enabled many workers in statutory and 'non-feminist' voluntary agencies to initiate discussions within their own workplace on a different, feminist policy and practice. From these initiatives have come suggestions for a feminist social work practice.

Protection work
Most concern and attention is devoted to the 'crisis of disclosure' – what to do when sexual abuse has been identified. This is not surprising; it is a crisis for all involved. Social workers who have a statutory duty to investigate *all* allegations of child abuse have to act to protect the child(ren) involved. This poses a painful dilemma: they *have* to act, often in the absence of clear ideas of what is the best thing to do, of training, and of the resources required to do the job. Teachers, nursery workers, health visitors and doctors usually work to guidelines which instruct them to inform social services but it is not compulsory for anyone to report abuse to 'the authorities' or the police.

Though this work is emotionally painful and demanding, it is not fundamentally different in the issues and dilemmas it raises from all other social work with children. Undertaking it well requires time, resources and good legal advice. Following disclosure, the aim is to ensure the safety of the child while decisions are made on how best to stop the abuse and help the child recover. If the abuser is a family member, this should be done by removing the abuser and not the child.

The focus of work must now be with mother, child, siblings and extended family. Two workers with a lot of time may be needed. (Some authorities now allow one worker to focus on work with the child and one to work with the mother.) The aim should be empowering the non-abusing adults, enabling the expression of feelings and encouraging emotional support for the child. Work of this quality cannot be done in agencies with no facilities for interviewing individuals and families in private, and with no resources for working with children. Adequate provision is not a priority for the present government.

Many mothers on learning of the abuse immediately assume responsibility for protecting the child. Some women are unable to do this. If their response is understood, and they are supported, then many more are able to make that choice. We are not suggesting that this is easy for either the mother or the worker, but the evidence is that it often does lead to a good outcome. If this cannot be achieved, then it may be possible to find an immediate safe solution within the framework of the wider family network, in order to avoid the need to remove the child. More resources are required to enable women to safeguard children: in

particular, the provision of refuges, including, where necessary, separate provision for Black women, or women from particular communities; legal advice for women and children; material support, and financial support for voluntary agencies which can offer help outside the umbrella of the state.

However, invoking statutory powers to protect children should not be seen as a sign of failure. Many survivors describe how they longed for someone to intervene to stop the abuse, and many children taken into care have been grateful. Public care can be a desperately inadequate solution for children, and it too often is; but it can and has been a refuge. Feminists need to begin thinking about what safe and good public care should be, and to work for change.

The second aspect of intervention which is widely discussed is the longer-term outcome. This is often posed as a question about the future of the 'whole family': will the 'family' break up, or is family rehabilitation possible? Most writers/commentators assume that to break up the family in any way is the worst thing that can happen to a child and is to be avoided at all costs. This was certainly voiced constantly in response to Cleveland. We are in no doubt that this is not true. To be abused by someone you love and trust, especially when he is your father, is worse, much worse, than family break-up. Separation of the child from the abuser does not have to mean that the child is immediately taken into care; if the family is not viewed in a monolithic way, then it is possible to distinguish between the abusing and non-abusing parts of the family.

Many women have to make an agonizing choice between their 'man' and their child, and this is a choice that they may need help to make. For some commentators, this is an unacceptable choice to pose to any woman. Here children's rights, which have been ignored in most of the post-Cleveland discussion, are central, and come into conflict with the rights of adults, about which we have heard so much. In this context we have no hesitation in putting the rights of children above the rights of adults, or the rights of women to choose who they live with or marry.

Survival
Protection and long-term arrangements are only one part of the process; there is also emotional work to be done with children, and we have argued that *how* you intervene to protect the child also has enormous implications for the process of emotional survival. There is of course

direct therapeutic work to be done at the time of disclosure. This is recognized by most professional workers, and there is agreement on many aspects. Specifically, it is agreed that the child must be believed, assured that it is not her/his fault, that s/he has been both brave and right to tell, and that s/he is not alone – that this has happened to other children too.

This formula is terribly important in conveying to children the way they are being perceived by 'authority', but it is not necessarily very effective in changing their perception of themselves. To avoid exacerbating the child's plight, workers must use their knowledge, their imagination and their own experiences of abuse and betrayal to enter into the child's world and to begin to judge what this abuse means for this child. This involves working directly with children and listening to them. The process of recovery is a long journey to which every bit of the child's current and future experience will contribute. Every intervention has to be thoroughly thought out and carefully executed. Some feminists argue that part of the abuse in all forms of sexual violence is the loss of control; emotional survival therefore depends on the abused woman or child being in control of what happens following disclosure. But child sexual abuse is an abuse of adult power, and many children have carried a dreadful burden of responsibility in protecting their abuser, themselves and their mother by keeping the secret. The experience of a positive use of adult power, of someone else making the decisions and taking the responsibility, may be very therapeutic. Children who have been abused have been deprived of their childhood; they need to be allowed to be dependent, so long as they are safe in that dependency. We cannot have absolute rules about how much control children and young people can take at different ages. It is a matter of delicate judgement.

Many people argue that to prosecute a man and to send him to prison only makes the child feel guilty or doubly punished. This may be the case if the child has to make that decision (as they do if they contact ChildLine). Part of the work that needs to be done with children at disclosure is to help them accept and understand their possibly ambivalent feelings towards their abuser, and that they are not in any way responsible for any consequences that follow for him. This is where a systems approach is particularly unhelpful in trying to see the family system as responsible. Blame is not a problematic emotion. We cannot sanitize what has happened. Someone has been wronged and somebody is blameworthy. Perhaps the most 'therapeutic' thing an abuser could do is to say, 'I was to blame; I shouldn't have done it.' They seldom do. Instead blame is taken by the child who, in the very confusion of her sexual desires and fantasies, is emotionally vulnerable to this. For a child who is sexually abused has a 'real' world within her fantasy world; undoing this requires the most careful and sensitive therapy.

The most important single contribution to recovery is changing the child's circumstances for the better, so that abuse is ended and the child is living with loving and caring adults, preferably those she already knows and loves, and if possible adults with whom she can talk about the abuse and her feelings. That children do survive without this does not affect its importance; we know that many don't.

Among feminists there are debates about what constitutes emotional survival and how best to achieve it. Incest survivors'/self-help groups have been an invaluable resource for many women, but for some they are only a first step. If survival is conceived as a long journey towards meaning, then it is clear that the theory underpinning any therapeutic work communicates meaning, and this has to be taken into account in assessing its effectiveness. Yet this is not done within non-feminist approaches. Therapy is never an equal relationship; there is always the possibility of the therapist abusing power. Such an abuse of power is never satisfactory, but in work with child and adult survivors it is disastrous. Those who offer therapy have a clear responsibility to examine the implications their theory has on meaning, and to examine rigorously their conduct and countertransference.

Thus within the orthodox approach, it is assumed that family therapy is useful in helping everyone to see what has gone wrong, assuming that abuse has happened because of family dynamics. However, it is probably most helpful in exposing the secret and facilitating discussion and negotiation about what is to happen. Similarly, it is assumed that group therapy for groups of abused children, for their mothers or for abusers is helpful in changing their perceptions of themselves, but depending upon how it is conducted (what theory informs the group leaders), it may merely confirm a whole range of disabling ideas about sexuality and parental roles. Finally, it is assumed that individual psychotherapy can help a survivor towards an understanding of the past, but it may merely exacerbate confusions about real and fantasy, desire and action, guilt and self-blame. Many workers claim that their approach is neutral; that it is not up to them to judge who is responsible or to blame. One cannot be theoretically neutral. We know, for example, that many survivors will feel that they are at least partly responsible, that perhaps they could have stopped it, that maybe their behaviour was interpreted by their abuser as consent. A therapist at this point has a choice: to ask in what way they feel responsible, or to ask whether they believe that a small child can consent.

Disclosing, talking, telling is important in challenging the power of the secret, of shame, in facing and confronting the pain, and in reaching catharsis, but it is not everything and it may not be enough. There have

to be a range of resources for self-help, therapy, and for women who need to 'breakdown' within a safe environment.

What is to be done about abusers?

In this account we, too, have concentrated on issues for children. The literature on child sexual abuse has astonishingly little to say about abusers. Whether he is described as a 'paedophile', a pitiful rejected husband, as the product of his own abused childhood, or as a sadistic brute, he is always described as being 'driven'. The fact that many abusers repeat their behaviour on other children leads orthodox therapists to use the term 'addiction' to describe the quality of obsession in this repetition. In the face of all this, there is a collective sense of helplessness. Many therapists, like those at the Portman Clinic in London, which specializes in work with sex offenders, continue in this difficult work as the only alternative to 'locking them up and throwing away the key'. While many feminists may feel that this is a good idea, or that it is 'not our problem', we cannot just leave it at that. While we argue for the removal of the abuser rather than the child from the home, many of these men will join or form new families and subsequently abuse other children.

Statutory workers will sometimes have to work with abusers, directly or as part of their work with children (for example, an abuser may be granted supervised access to his child(ren)). Within the orthodox framework, children will be expected to be part of family meetings with their abuser, and they propose that abusers, prior to family rehabilitation, must not only accept their responsibility for what they have done but must say so to their child. We do not believe that children should *have* to experience this; but some children will want to see/have contact with their abuser, and workers will have to handle this.

The first questions usually posed about abusers are whether criminal proceedings are the appropriate way of dealing with sexual offences against children and young people, and whether abusers should be sent to prison. Arguments for decriminalization come from a very wide range of people – from those who argue that it is a 'family matter'; from those who believe that it punishes a child still further; from those who argue that the 'punitive' climate is preventing abusers from admitting their guilt; and from those who believe that prosecution and prison will achieve nothing whereas therapy might.

There are three separate aspects to this issue: the impact on the meaning of the event; the impact on the children involved, and the best way of changing abusers. Of the first we are in no doubt: to decriminalize child sexual abuse is to say that it is not very serious; it is to support the idea that abusers are pathetic or disturbed, and certainly not responsible for their actions. Child sexual abuse, like rape and domestic violence, must be seen as a straightforward crime against the person. Anything else is an injustice to those assaulted. While it is clear that prison is not successful at reforming anyone, to abandon it for sexual offences (before, for example, crimes against property) is to regard sexual offences as a special category of behaviour and to collude with the notion of men's 'uncontrollable drive'. While many abusers, having internalized the ideology, may perceive themselves thus, it is quite wrong for the state to concur. Finally, a custodial sentence does guarantee the safety of women and children for a period of time.

The second argument looks at the impact on children, arguing that children's feelings of self-blame are worsened by the responsibility they feel for sending their father to prison. Without wishing to play down the pain of this, we believe that children can be helped to deal with it. Moreover, this view takes account of only *one* aspect of a child's painfully ambivalent feelings at this time. One way of helping a child not to feel responsible may be for society to say clearly: 'He is responsible.' Survivors' accounts demonstrate both their ambivalence, and their desire to see their abuser punished in some way: 'I hated him and I wanted him punished, but he was my father and I loved him' (Channel 4, 1984), said one adult woman of her distress as a child giving evidence against her father. Clearly the debates on these questions will continue; we have to be sure that our arguments about what should be done do not come from *denial*, from an inability to face up to and accept the reality and seriousness of child sexual abuse.

Finally, what about changing men? It is true that prison, as currently organized, is not very effective at changing men's behaviour; but then neither is therapy. 'There can be little question that the strongest predictor of future sexual offences is past sexual offences' (Dreiblatt, 1982: 3). This is not surprising. If therapy is also a search for meaning, then much of it confirms, rather than challenges, their own story to themselves: they have an overwhelming obsession; they are

lonely, rejected, unhappy. Traditional approaches to 'treatment' may not be useful:

> Mental health practitioners are trained to adopt a helping, accepting and caring posture. They are discouraged from taking an authoritative and controlling stance. The mental health approach emphasizes client support: one attempts to trust and believe one's client and have confidence in him. Although not completely so, this posture is the antithesis of the authority-based treatment approach one takes with a sex offender. Effective assessment and treatment of the offender requires a degree of skepticism and cynicism on the part of the professional. I tell my clients that I do not operate on a trust basis. Trust is what is abusable. I communicate to them that I have no intention of feeling confident in them. Feeling confident in them can be dangerous. (Dreiblatt, 1982: 3)

What is required is something altogether more bracing, less collusive and more challenging, aimed at exploring power, anger and fear, more than sex, love and desire:

> A direct, focused approach to the offence . . . confrontative and challenging . . . Although we are often taught to focus on *why* behaviour has occurred, your assessment will be more effective if you focus on *what* has happened. The tough-minded approach. (Dreiblatt, 1982: 5)

Until and unless it is recognized that child sexual abuse is a gender issue, and a product of the social construction of masculinity, there can be no change, either in individual men or in masculinity, no counter to the dominant messages, no way of providing boys with an alternative view of masculinity. Posing an alternative explanation of child sexual abuse, and giving it a different meaning, is an essential part of the wider political struggle towards real prevention.

Training, prevention and the way forward

The little money available for child sexual abuse work from this close-fisted government is for training and prevention. These are the way forward say the establishment; but its conception of training and prevention are a monument to the wrong-headedness of the theory. There are to be more specialist workers, more specialist units in the orthodox mould; and children are to be taught how to say 'no' to sexual assault by special programmes developed for use in schools: 'My body's nobody's body but mine', say the eager children in a Rolf Harris video. 'Please leave it alone when you hear me say 'No!'[1]

There is nothing wrong or malevolent about the desire to do something; nothing wrong with wanting to help children be more assertive; nothing wrong in trying to improve, through wide training, the service to children and families. However, if the problem of

masculinity is edited out of the discourse on child sexual abuse, we are left with children waging a war armed only with words, the adults having left the front. As this issue of *Feminist Review* and all the other feminist writings on child sexual abuse show, we do have ideas, resources, possibilities, weapons for a different fight, aimed at transforming knowledge and instituting a different practice.

Notes

Mary MacLeod and Esther Saraga teach social work and psychology respectively at the Polytechnic of North London, where they have recently established a Child Abuse Studies Unit.

We would like to thank all the women with whom we have discussed these ideas. Drawings by Kerry.

1 Chorus and one of the verses from 'My Body' by Peter Alsop, sung in the video *Kids Can Say No!* produced by Rolf Harris Video, 43 Drury Lane, London WC2B 5RT.

References

ANGELOU, Maya (1984) *I Know Why the Caged Bird Sings* London: Virago Press.

ASH, Angie (1984) *Father-Daughter Sexual Abuse: The Abuse of Paternal Authority* Bangor: University College of North Wales.

BAILLIE, Beverley (1983) 'All For the Love of Ann' *Community Care* no. 489.

BAKER, Anthony W. and DUNCAN, Sylvia P. (1985) 'Child Sexual Abuse: A Study of Prevalence in Great Britain' *Child Abuse and Neglect* Vol. 9, pp. 457–67.

BAKER, Tony and DUNCAN, Sylvia (1986) 'Child Sexual Abuse' in MEADOW (1986).

BOGRAD, Michele (1984) 'Family Systems Approaches to Wife Battering: A Feminist Critique' *American Journal of Orthopsychiatry* Vol, 54, no. 4.

CAMERON, Deborah and FRAZER, Elizabeth (1987) *The Lust to Kill* Cambridge: Polity Press.

CHANNEL 4 (1984) 'Child Sex Abuse' Programme 1: 'The Evidence' 20/20 Vision.

CLARK, Anna (1987) *Women's Silence: Men's Violence* London: Pandora Press.

COOK, Mark and HOWELLS, Kevin (1981) *Adult Sexual Interest in Children* London: Academic Press.

DAVIS, Angela Y. (1985) *Violence Against Women and the Ongoing Challenge to Racism* Latham, NY: Kitchen Table/Women of Color Press.

DOMINELLI, Lena (1986) 'Father–Daughter Incest: Patriarchy's Shameful Secret' *Critical Social Policy* no. 16.

DREIBLATT, Irwin S. (1982) *Issues in the Evaluation of the Sex Offender* A Presentation at The Washington State Psychological Association Meetings.

FREUD, Anna (1981) 'A Psychoanalyst's View of Sexual Abuse by Parents' in MRAZEK and KEMPE (1981).

FINKELHOR, David (1979) *Sexually Victimized Children* London: Free Press.

FROSH, Stephen (1987) 'Issues for Men Working with Sexually Abused Children' *British Journal of Psychotherapy* Vol. 3, no. 4.

GORDON, Linda (1985) 'Child Abuse, Gender and the Myth of Family Independence: A Historical Critique' *Child Welfare* Vol. LXIV, no. 3.

HEATH, Stephen (1982) *The Sexual Fix* London: Macmillan.

HERMAN, Judith Lewis (1981) *Father–Daughter Incest* London: Harvard.

HILDEBRAND, Judy and FORBES, Constanze (1987) 'Group Work with Mothers Whose Children Have Been Sexually Abused' *British Journal of Social Work* Vol. 17, pp. 285–304.

KEMPE, Ruth S. and KEMPE, C. Henry (1978) *Child Abuse* London: Fontana/Open Books.

KEMPE, Ruth S. and KEMPE, C. Henry (1984) *The Common Secret* New York: Freeman.

KINSEY, Alfred C. et al. (1948) *Sexual Behaviour in the Human Male* Philadelphia: Saunders.

KINSEY, Alfred C. et al. (1953) *Sexual Behaviour in the Human Female* Philadelphia: Saunders.

LANGFELDT, Thore (1981) 'Sexual Development in Children' in COOK and HOWELLS (1981).

LONDON RAPE CRISIS CENTRE (1984) *Sexual Violence* London: The Women's Press.

LONDON RAPE CRISIS CENTRE (1987) *Strength in Numbers* London: London Rape Crisis Centre.

MEADOW, Roy (1986) *Recent Advances in Paediatrics* Edinburgh: Churchill Livingstone.

MRAZEK, Patricia Beezley and BENTOVIM, Arnon (1981) 'Incest and the Dysfunctional Family System' in MRAZEK and KEMPE (1981).

MRAZEK, Patricia Beezley and KEMPE, C. Henry (1981) *Sexually Abused Children and their Families* Oxford: Pergamon Press.

NASH, C. L. and WEST, D. J. (1985) 'Sexual Molestation of Young Girls: A Retrospective Survey' in WEST (1985).

NELSON, Sarah (1982, 1987) *Incest: Fact and Myth* Edinburgh: Stramullion.

NSPCC South West Region Working Party (1984) *Developing a Child Centred Response to Sexual Abuse* London: NSPCC.

O'CARROLL, Tom (1980) *Paedophilia: The Radical Case* London: Peter Owen.

OWEN, Marika (1987) 'Laying Ghosts to Rest' *Community Care* no. 643.

PARTON, Nigel (1985) *The Politics of Child Abuse* London: Macmillan.

PILAIS, Jennie and ANDERTON, Joy (1986) 'Feminism and Family Therapy – A Possible Meeting Point' *Journal of Family Therapy* Vol. 8, no. 2.

PLUMMER, Ken (1981) 'Pedophilia: Constructing a Sociological Baseline' in COOK and HOWELLS (1981).

PORTER, Ruth (1984) editor *Child Sexual Abuse Within the Family* London: Tavistock/CIBA Foundation.

RUSH, Florence (1980) *The Best Kept Secret* New York: McGraw-Hill.

RUSSELL, Diana E. H. (1984) *Sexual Exploitation* London: Sage.

RUSSELL, Diana E. H. (1986) *The Secret Trauma* New York: Basic Books.

SEABROOKE, Jeremy (1987) 'The Corruption of Childhood' *New Statesman* Vol. 114, no. 2937.

SOPHOCLES (1947) *The Theban Plays* Harmondsworth: Penguin.

WATTENBERG, Esther (1985) 'In a Different Light: A Feminist Perspective on the Role of Mothers in Father-Daughter Incest' *Child Welfare* Vol. LXIV, no. 3.

WEEKS, Jeffrey (1985) *Sexuality and its Discontents* London: Routledge & Kegan Paul.

WEIR, Kirk (1987) 'Report of AFT Research Meeting: June 1987' *Association of Family Therapists Newsletter* Vol. 7, no. 3.

WEST, D. J. 'Adult Sexual Interest in Children: Implications for Social Control' in COOK and HOWELLS (1981).

WEST, D. J. (1985) editor *Sexual Victimization* Aldershot: Gower.

WINNICOTT, Donald (1961) *Home is Where We Start From* Harmondsworth: Penguin.

THE POLITICS OF CHILD SEXUAL ABUSE:
Notes from American History

Linda Gordon

In the early 1970s, when a radical feminist consciousness pulled incest out of the closet, we thought we were engaged in an unprecedented discovery. In fact, charity volunteers and social workers a century earlier dealt with incest cases daily, understanding them to be a standard, expected part of the caseload of a child-protective agency such as a Society for the Prevention of Cruelty to Children. How are we to explain this historical amnesia? Like the suppression of so much women's history and feminist analysis, this hiatus was not created simply by the decline in feminism between 1920 and 1970, but by an active reinterpretation of child sexual abuse. I shudder when I think about what this meant: not only because of the incest victims rendered invisible and mute, but also because of its threat to us today, the threat that great achievements in consciousness-raising can be rolled back by powerful ideological tanks. My motives in writing a history of family violence were thus far from disinterested.[1]

Charity and social workers in the late nineteenth-century United States were familiar with child sexual abuse and knew that its most common form of abuse was intrafamilial – that is, incest. Ten per cent of the family-violence case records of Boston child-saving agencies which I sampled, starting in 1880, contained incest (Gordon and O'Keefe, 1986; Gordon, 1984). Moreover, in their upper-class way these child savers had a feminist analysis of the problem: they blamed male brutality and lack of sexual control. They could safely offer such explanations because they believed the problem to occur exclusively among the Catholic immigrant poor, whom they perceived as of 'inferior stock', crowded 'like animals' into urban ghettoes. Thus, ironically, the very upper-class base of child-rescue work at the time promoted the identification of problems unmentionable by standards of Victorian propriety.

Despite these class limitations, the sympathy for child victims entailed by this sensibility was one of the major achievements of the nineteenth-century feminist movement. The attack on male sexual and familial violence was often disguised in temperance rhetoric. American women's historians have recently conducted a reinterpretation of temperance, acknowledging its anti-Catholic, anti-working class content, but also identifying its meanings for women contesting the evils that alcohol created for them and their families: violence, disease, impoverishment, male irresponsibility. Moreover, the feminist anti-violence campaign had significant successes. In the course of the century wife-beating was transformed from an acceptable practice into one which, despite its continued widespread incidence, was illegal and reprehensible, a seamy behaviour which men increasingly denied and tried to hide (Pleck, 1979). Indeed, the whole movement against child abuse which began in the 1870s was a product of a feminist sensibility in several ways: first, in opposing corporal punishment and preference for gentler methods of child training; second, in challenging the sanctity of the Victorian home and authority of the paterfamilias. Most manuals of child raising by the last quarter of the nineteenth century recommended physical punishment only as a last resort, and women's legal victories in child custody created a preference for maternal rights to children for a century.

Consider a few examples of incest cases from the late nineteenth century:[2]

> In 1900 a thirteen year old girl has been placed out with a family in which the wife is absent. The SPCC worker reports that the 'child's bed not slept in but [the father's bed is] much tumbled. The girl cries and dreads the night.' (Case #1820A)

> An incest victim reports, sometime in the 1890s, that her father 'told her that it was all right for him to do such things and say such things to her, for all fathers did so with their daughters. Tried to force her to go to a hotel in Boston with him once. Also advised her to go with fellows to get money. Said that if she got in trouble he would help her out . . . .' (Case #2058A)

There were hundreds of these stories telling us not only that incest occurred, but that child-saving agencies were aware of it and taking action against it. The publicity and fund-raising efforts of the Massachusetts Society for the Prevention of Cruelty to Children focussed on intrafamily 'carnal abuse' directly, unembarrassed to include it as part of the need for SPCC intervention.

In the early twentieth century the child-savers' view of child sexual assault changed significantly, and incest was de-emphasized. By the 1920s, although child-protective agencies continued to meet many incest cases, a three-part interpretive transformation had occurred: the *locus* of the problem was moved from home to streets, the *culprit* transformed from father or other authoritative male family member to perverted stranger, the *victim* transformed from innocent betrayed to sex delinquent. In other words, the fact that child sex abuse is over-whelmingly a family problem was obscured; instead it was pictured as rape by strangers on the streets. (Anna Clark has shown how a similar reinterpretation of adult rape took place (Clark, 1987).) This is not to say that there was no extrafamilial sex abuse; there was, but, compared to incest, it was greatly exaggerated in both public and professional discourse.

Several factors contributed to this reinterpretation. The profes-sionalization of social work tended to weaken the influence of feminists and social reformers among child protectors, even as, ironically, more women entered child welfare casework as salaried workers. After the women's suffrage victory in 1920 the organized feminist movement fragmented and weakened. During World War I venereal disease became a major problem for the armed forces (it was for this reason that condoms became widely available at this time, first issued by the Navy to sailors); servicemen were presented as victims of disease-ridden prostitutes. After the war, fears of Bolshevism, sexual freedom, and feminism combined to create a 'pro-family' backlash.

The implications of this reinterpretation of child sexual abuse were pernicious for women and girls. The existence of sexual abuse became evidence requiring the constriction and domestication of girls, and their mothers were blamed for inadequate supervision if the girls were molested or even played on the streets. What was once categorized as carnal abuse, the perpetrators virtually all male, was often now cate-gorized as moral neglect – meaning that the mother was the culprit and the behaviour of the victim was implicated. Some of the 'sex abuse' was relatively noncoercive teenage sexuality. Female juvenile sex delin-quency was constructed as a major social problem in early twentieth-century America, and it was a vague, victimless crime. Girls who smoked and drank, dressed or spoke immodestly, or simply loitered on the streets were convicted of sex delinquency in substantial numbers and sent to reformatories (Schlossman and Wallach, 1978). During World War I near armed-forces bases it was the servicemen who were the innocents, their girl partners the sources of pollution. Even girls who had been raped were no longer victims but temptresses. I do not mean to deny that some girls behaved in socially dangerous and self-destructive ways, nor that they sought out sexual adventure but, as many students of sex delinquents and other runaways today have observed, high proportions, quite possibly a majority of these girls, were first victims of sexual assault, typically familial. They were, so to speak, squeezed out onto the streets in search of safety and/or self-esteem from homes that were even more destructive than the street boys or men who exploited them.

Above all, this reinterpretation of child sexual abuse removed scrutiny from family and home, restoring the curtain of impunity that surrounded those sacred institutions. This was the period of the discovery of the 'dirty old man', the 'sex fiend', and the 'pervert', the stereotypical culprit in child sex abuse cases in the 1930s, 1940s and 1950s. As before, I do not wish to deny that such figures existed. Child protection agencies uncovered child prostitution, pornography rings and sex criminals who molested literally scores of children. The victims were not always brutalized; the children of the very poor – not only in the Depression but in earlier decades too – could be bribed into acquiescence and silence with a nickel, an orange, a pail of coal. However, even these nonfamilial molesters were rarely 'strangers'. They were often neighbours, accepted members of communities, often small businessmen or janitors who had access to private space.

There were two peak periods of hysteria about sex crimes: 1937–40 and 1949–55. The panic had official government sponsorship, led by none less that J. Edgar Hoover, head of the FBI. In 1937 he called for a 'War on the Sex Criminal'. Hoover's rantings about 'degenerates' threatening 'American childhood and womanhood' assimilated these sexual anxieties to nationalism, racism and anti-Communism. It bears notice that, in contrast to earlier periods of public agitation against sex crimes, as in campaigns to raise the age of consent in the Progressive era, women's organizations played no role in this campaign (Freedman, 1987).

Meanwhile social workers became less likely to investigate girls' typically euphemistic accusations of their fathers.

> In 1935 a mother turned her daughter in for sex delinquency. Investigation reveals that the daughter, fleeing from an abusive father, who also beat his wife severely, had spent most of her time for 4–5 years with her maternal uncle and aunt. She accused her maternal uncle of molesting her steadily. However, the MSPCC physical exam indicated that she was a virgin,[3] so no action was taken. (#3555A)

> A battered woman, terrified of her husband, is told by their daughter, who has become a 'sex delinquent,' behaving 'vulgarly,' that her father has criminally assaulted her. The mother says 'she would speak to him.' At court the police chief says he is doubtful about taking up the case as the girl's word is the only evidence the Government could produce; he would not question the father 'as it would be asking [him] to incriminate himself.' The daughter was committed to an institution.(#2057A)

> In 1920 a mother is so fearful that her new husband will abuse her daughter (from a previous marriage) that every time she goes out she hires a babysitter to chaperone them. Yet when the daughter, now eleven, says she has been raped by a 'stranger' whom she refuses to name, the social workers not only fail to question whether she might be shielding her stepfather, but decide that her accusation is not credible and brand her a delinquent – a liar, immoral, and uncontrollable. She is boarded out as a domestic. (#3085A)

> In 1930 a 14-year-old girl alleges sexual abuse by her widowed father and
> begs to be taken out of his home. No action is taken until the father brings
> her to court on stubborn-child charges and she, as well as her younger
> sister whom she has been trying to protect are sentenced, separately, to
> institutions. (#3585)

In addition to references like these, in which the agencies did not
investigate or prosecute, there were many others in which agency
workers simply did not pick up the broad hints that girls threw out,
hoping to draw attention to their plight. Social workers ignored statements like, 'I asked my mother for a lock on my door'. These girls were
not usually bribed or intimidated into silence. Some of the recent
discussion of incest emphasizes victims' fearful silence, but this evidence is based on the work of therapists, counselling incest victims
years later, who have often by then reconstructed their stories on the
basis of their guilt; my evidence, contemporaneous with the abuse,
showed that these children were usually very active in trying to get help,
more so, for example, than victims of nonsexual child abuse (Gordon,
1986).

Not only did social workers de-emphasize incest, but academic
experts dismissed it as an extremely rare, one-in-a-million occurrence
(Weinberg, 1955). Psychoanalytic and anthropological interpretations,
associated respectively with Freud and Lévi-Strauss, attributed to
incest taboos a vital role in the development of civilization; this logic
brought with it the assumption that these taboos were effective and that
incest was, in fact, rare; but in terms of impact on treatment of actual
cases, Freudian thought did not so much *cause* social workers to deny
children's complaints and hints about sexual mistreatment as it offered
categories with which to explain away these complaints. As Boston
psychiatrist Eleanor Pavenstedt commented in 1954:

> Most of us have trained ourselves to skepticism toward the claims of
> young girls who maintain they have been seduced by their fathers . . . We
> must ask ourselves whether our tendency to disbelief is not in part at
> least based on denial. The incest barrier is perhaps the strongest support
> of our cultural family structure, and we may well shrink from the thought
> of its being threatened. (Pavenstedt, 1954)

So did the dominant sociology of the family, which inverted Lévi-
Strauss's functionalism to prove that the incest taboo was operative
because it had to be. For example, 'No known human society could
tolerate much incest without ruinous disruption' (Gebhard, Gagnon,
Pomeroy and Christenson, 1965: 208; Davis, 1949; Bell and Vogel,
1963). The few nonfeminist historians to study incest replicated that
error by studying public beliefs about incest, not behaviour (Wohl, 1979;
Strong, 1973).

The rediscovery of incest in the 1970s was, then, merely a reinterpretation, and it did not come quickly. Nonsexual child abuse was

resurrected as a social problem in the 1960s in a movement led by physicians but stimulated by the influence of the New Left, with its sympathy for youth and critique of authority and the family. Without pressure from feminists, incest first reappeared as gender-neutral. Indeed, the very classification of all forms of intrafamily sexual activity as incest obscures the meanings of these behaviours. For example, sibling sexual activity, or sex between other relatives of approximately the same age, is extremely common, difficult to identify and not necessarily abusive. Mother–child incest is extremely rare and, in my findings, more often than father–child incest, associated with adult mental illness; by contrast incestuous fathers have extremely 'normal' profiles (Gordon and O'Keefe, 1984; Herman, 1981). Yet many child abuse experts throughout the 1970s ignored these gender differences (Kempe, 1980; Money, 1980). Others found ingenious ways of explaining away actuality with speculation about possibility. Thus social worker Kate Rist argued that 'society has created a stronger prohibition against mother-son incest' because 'it is most likely to occur. This has led to the intriguing situation in which father-daughter incest appears to have a lower natural probability of occurrence, is therefore less strongly prohibited, and in practice occurs more often' (Rist, 1979; 682).

Historians do not usually like to speak of the 'lessons of history', as if she were some objective, finally definitive schoolteacher. But in many years of work at the craft, I have never come across a story that so directly yields a moral. The moral is that the presence or absence of a strong feminist movement makes the difference between better and worse solutions to the social problem of child sexual abuse; more, that the very same evidence of sexual abuse will be differently defined in the presence or absence of that movement. Without a feminist analysis, evidence of child sexual abuse means that danger lies in sex perverts, in public spaces, in unsupervised girls, in sexually assertive girls. There are few ironies more bitter than the fact that rape of children – that most heinous of crimes – has also been the crime most drenched in victim-blaming. As with adult rape, child sexual abuse without feminist interpretation supplies evidence and arguments for constricting and disempowering children.

Such a reinterpretation arose again in the United States in the mid-1980s, a reinterpretation aided, of course, by the real and increasing incidence of deranged killers attacking strangers. In the school year 1984/85 my then second-grade daughter was taught *three* separate programmes in her classroom about how to react to sexual abuse attempts, all of them emphasizing strangers, and all of them gender-neutral. The most publicized sexual abuse cases have concerned daycare centres, and often female teachers, although daycare centres remain, on the whole, among the safest environments for children. The statistics about child sexual abuse remain what they were a century ago: the most dangerous place for children is the home, the most likely assailant their father. Similarly a panic about missing children not only exaggerated their numbers a thousandfold, but completely misstated the source of such 'kidnappings': neglecting to mention that noncustodial parents are overwhelmingly the main kidnappers; and that teenage runaways, often from abusive homes, are overwhelmingly the majority of the missing children.

What then is the best policy? My argument should not be taken as an implicit call for de-emphasizing the problem. On the contrary. The children's educational programmes and pamphlets have strengths, particularly in so far as they offer assertiveness training for children: if it feels uncomfortable, trust your judgement and say no; scream loud and run fast; tell someone. Of course it is difficult and inadvisable to sow distrust of fathers, particularly because the more intimate fathers are with children, the more responsibility they have for children, the less likely they will be to abuse them sexually. However, education for children should contain a feminist and an anti-authoritarian analysis: should discuss the relative powerlessness of women and girls, and praise assertiveness and collective resistance in girls; should demystify the family and even discuss that ultimately tabooed subject, economic power in the family. Education for boys must be equally brave and delicate. Boys are children too, and often victimized sexually, but they are also future men, and school age is not too early to ask them to consider what's wrong with male sexual aggression, to teach them to criticize the multiple and powerful cultural messages that endorse male sexual aggression.

Probably the most important single contribution to the prevention of incest would be the strengthening of mothers. By increasing their ability to support themselves and their social and psychological self-esteem, allowing them to choose independence if that is necessary to protect themselves and their daughters, men's sexual exploitation could be checked. In the historical incest cases I sampled, one of the most consistent common denominators was the extreme helplessness of mothers – often the victims of wife-beating themselves, they were often ill or otherwise isolated, they were the poorest, the least self-confident and the least often employed of mothers in these case records. This is not victim-blaming; their weaknesses were not their fault, but part of the systematic way in which male supremacy gives rise to incest. It was a gain that wife-beating and incest have become more criminalized, but we cannot expect women to prosecute aggressively if their prospects for single motherhood are so bleak.

Moreover, women's very subordination often contributes to making them child abusers and neglecters. Although women do not usually abuse children sexually, in these case records they were responsible for approximately half the nonsexual child abuse (the same proportion they occupy in many contemporary studies). Unfortunately, feminists have avoided women's own violence towards children and analysed family violence in terms of stereotypical male brutality and female gentleness. Women's violence should not be regarded as a problem that will somehow weaken our feminist claims; on the contrary, these claims should not rest on assumptions of women's superiority – those of us who behave worst may be those who need empowerment mòst. Women's mistreatment of children also needs an analysis of the damages caused by the sexual division of labour and the pattern of women's exclusive responsibility for child-raising. In the US, too, the rather middle-class radical feminist groups never made issues of social services a political priority, although such services are fundamental to women's ability to resist violence, to protect their children, and to parent better themselves.

This is not to say that a good feminist line will solve the problems of child sexual abuse, expecially not where the abuse has already occurred. Like everyone else, feminists who deal with policy or individual cases must wobble through many contradictions. For example: the victimization is real, but the tendency to exaggerate its incidence and to produce social and moral panics needs to be resisted. The problem emerges from the powerlessness, the effective invisibility and muteness of women and children, especially girls, but the adult anxiety has led to children's false accusations, and children's sufferings will not be corrected by eroding the due process rights and civil liberties of those accused. Child sexual abuse needs a political interpretation, in terms of male power. However, the prosecution of culprits – however necessary – and the breaking up of families that may result do not always benefit the child victims. Especially if they are incestuous, sex abuse cases have something of the tragic about them, because once they arise, tremendous human damage has already occurred, and a politically correct analysis will not ease the pain. Still, that analysis, situating the problem in the context of male supremacy in and outside the family, is the only long-term hope for prevention.

Notes

Linda Gordon is Professor of History at the University of Wisconsin/Madison. She is the author of *Woman's Body, Woman's Right* and the forthcoming book on family violence noted below.

1 My book, *Heroes of Their Own Lives: The History and Politics of Family Violence*, is forthcoming from Viking/Penguin US in early 1988. References to my sources and more information on my research methodology can be found there.
2 These and other excerpts are from case records of Boston, Massachusetts, child-protection agencies (see Gordon, 1988).
3 The standard response to a sex abuse allegation was to look at the condition of the hymen (Gordon, 1988).

References

BELL, Norman and VOGEL, Ezra (1963) editors *A Modern Introduction to the Family* New York: Free Press.

BREINES, Wini and GORDON, Linda (1983) 'The New Scholarship on Family Violence' *Signs* 8, pp. 490–531.

CLARK, Anna (1987) *Women's Silence, Men's Violence: Sexual Assault in England 1770–1845* London: Pandora Press.

DAVIS, Kingsley (1949) *Human Society* New York: Macmillan.

DUBOIS, Ellen and GORDON, Linda (1983) 'Seeking Ecstasy on the Battlefield: Danger and Pleasure in Nineteenth-century Feminist Sexual Thought' *Feminist Studies* 9, pp. 7–25; also *Feminist Review* no. 11 (1981).

FREEDMAN, Estelle B. (1987) "Uncontrolled Desires": The Response to the Sexual Psychopath, 1920–1960' *Journal of American History* Vol. 74, no. 1, pp. 83–106.

GEBHARD, Paul, GAGNON, J. POMEROY, Wardell and CHRISTENSON, C. (1965) *Sex Offenders* New York: Harper & Row.

GORDON, Linda and O'KEEFE, Paul (1984) 'Incest as a Form of Family Violence: Evidence from Historical Case Records' *Journal of Marriage and the Family* Vol. 46, no. 1, pp. 27–34.

GORDON, Linda (1986) 'Incest and Resistance: Patterns of Father-Daughter Incest, 1880–1930' *Social Problems* Vol. 33, no. 4, pp. 253–67.

GORDON, Linda (1988) *Heroes of Their Own Lives: The Politics and History of Family Violence* New York: Viking/Penguin.

HERMAN, Judith (1981) *Father-Daughter Incest* Cambridge: Harvard University Press.

KAUFMAN, Irving, PECK, Alice L. and TAGIURI, Consuelo K. (1954) 'The Family Constellation and Overt Incestuous Relations Between Father and Daughter' *American Journal of Orthopsychiatry* Vol. 24, pp. 266—79.

KEMPE, C. Henry (1980) 'Incest and Other Forms of Sexual Abuse' in KEMPE (1980).

KEMPE, C. Henry and HELFER, Ray (1980) *The Battered Child* Chicago: University of Chicago Press.

MONEY, John, (1980) Introduction to the incest section in WILLIAMS and MONEY (1980).

PAVENSTEDT, Eleanor (1954) Addendum to KAUFMAN, PECK and TAGIURI (1954).

PLECK, Elizabeth (1979) 'Wife Beating in Nineteenth-century America' *Victimology* Vol. 4, no. 1, pp. 60–74.

RIST, Kate (1979) 'Incest: Theoretical and Clinical Views' *American Journal of Orthopsychiatry* Vol. 49, no. 4, pp. 680–91.

RUSH, Florence (1980) *The Best Kept Secret: Sexual Abuse of Children* Englewood Cliffs, NJ: Prentice-Hall.

SCHLOSSMAN, Steven and WALLACH, Stephanie (1978) 'The Crime of Precocious Sexuality: Female Juvenile Delinquency in the Progressive Era' *Harvard Educational Review* 48, pp. 65–94.

STRONG, Bryan (1973) 'Toward a History of the Experiential Family: Sex and Incest in the Nineteenth-century Family' *Journal of Marriage and the Family*, Vol. 35, no. 3, pp. 457–66.

WEINBERG, S. (1955) *Incest Behavior* New York: Citadel Press.

WILLIAMS, Gertrude J. and MONEY, John (1980) editors *Traumatic Abuse and Neglect of Children at Home* Baltimore: Johns Hopkins.

WOHL, Anthony S. (1979) 'Sex and the Single Room: Incest Among the Victorian Working Classes' in *The Victorian Family: Structure and Stress* ed. Wohl. New York: St Martin's Press.

WHAT'S IN A NAME?:
Defining Child Sexual Abuse

Liz Kelly

What strikes me as the most bizarre aspect of the 'Cleveland crisis', and the debate surrounding it, is the transformation of the meaning of the term 'sexual abuse' in public discourse. Whilst feminists have been arguing for years that children are sexually abused inside the home as well as outside it, I don't think we could have envisaged the shift in public perceptions to the extent that, in the United Kingdom, child sexual abuse has currently become synonymous with incest. The most obvious recent example being the assertion by the head of Cleveland Social Services that if his department has evidence that a child has been sexually abused they have no choice but to remove the child from the home. Apart from begging the question of alternative intervention strategies – particularly the removal of the abuser from the household – this is an extremely strange statement for those of us whose definition of child sexual abuse includes assaults by strangers, sexual harassment and flashing.

My initial outline for this article involved contrasting feminist definitions of child sexual abuse – which I took to be broader and based on what women and girls experience as abusive – with narrower 'expert' definitions currently influencing professional practice. The more I thought about these issues, though, the more I realized that similar confusions exist within our own writing and service work. We too are beginning to use the term 'sexual abuse' to refer only to incestuous abuse; we too are getting caught up in using incidence figures inappropriately. Whilst there are no simple solutions to the question of how we define terms, as these issues are as much political as they are linguistic, there are some ways in which greater clarity is both possible and necessary.

For instance, Stuart Bell (the Labour MP who has played a central role in the 'Cleveland crisis') has stated on a number of occasions that 'there is no evidence' to support the prevalence figures used in a Cleveland Social Services discussion document (that is, one in four girls and one in ten boys). His comment was repeated as an authoritative 'fact' in a number of subsequent television news stories and discussion programmes on child sexual abuse. My immediate reaction to these comments was that yet again evidence even from carefully conducted research is not accepted when it involves sexual violence of any kind. I still suspect that Stuart Bell has never studied the incidence research that is available, but I have come to see that his comments highlight a more important general point – the confusion that is created when complex research and analysis is oversimplified and used inappropriately.

These prevalence figures are confirmed (and in some cases exceeded) by carefully conducted studies in the US and the UK (Finkelhor, 1979; Hall, 1985; Russell, 1984; West, 1985), but each of these studies covers intra- and extra-familial forms of child sexual abuse. Whilst the figures have become widely known, the research and definitions of child sexual abuse on which they were based have not. In the current climate they are read, and are indeed on occasions used, as figures about incest. I am beginning to wonder whether some of the disbelief and denial that many of us working in this area encounter is, in fact, based on this misunderstanding. Further confusion arises when, in attempting to get the issue of child sexual abuse on the public agenda, the likelihood of a child experiencing some form of sexual abuse before the age of sixteen is transformed into numbers of children currently being abused or who will experience abuse in any one year.

I am not raising these issues because I agree with the 'moral panic' argument; I will suggest later that sexual abuse of girls is more prevalent than the 'one in four' figure. Rather, I want to point out how easily our work can be undermined if we are not clear about the terms we use or what figures based on research studies actually mean. What I want to do in this article is use evidence from my own research on sexual violence (Kelly, 1986) to explore how limited definitions work to exclude what women and girls actually experience as abusive. I shall then outline the parameters of a feminist definition of sexual abuse and conclude with some comments on the implications of this discussion for feminist theory and practice.

There is a theoretical issue which underpins my approach, which I want briefly to outline at this point. It has been an important principle of feminist scholarship in relation to both sexual violence and language that we name our own experience. This has required both that we challenge dominant definitions and meanings (for example, of rape) and that we introduce new words which reflect women's experience (for example, sexual harassment). In this process feminists have extended the definitions of words we ourselves introduced as we discovered and documented the range of sexual violence. There are some forms of feminist redefinition, however, which I feel are less helpful. The collapsing of all forms of sexual assault into 'rape' in the most recent report from London Rape Crisis (LRC, 1987) and the similar catch-all use of sexual harassment by Sue Wise and Liz Stanley (Wise and Stanley, 1987) creates the same kind of confusion as the reducing of child sexual abuse to incest. There is an important difference between extending definitions in order to reflect the complexity of experience and collapsing a number of forms of sexual violence into one category. Taking the latter route means we lose the possibility of exploring just what the similarities and differences between various forms of sexual violence are. At the same time, however, it is important to acknowledge that straightforward analytic definitions are equally problematic. Firstly, because forms of sexual violence shade into one another at certain points. Secondly, how women define their experiences of sexual violence varies, both between women and over time for any individual woman (Kelly, forthcoming). Conceptualizing sexual violence as a continuum is one way of reflecting both the problems of defining forms of sexual violence and the complexity of women's experience (Kelly, 1987).

Researching sexual violence

I interviewed sixty women and asked them if they had ever experienced a number of forms of sexual violence. In the interviews I tried not to presume shared definitions: for example, I asked if women had had a negative sexual experience in childhood and/or adolescence rather than asking if they had ever been sexually abused; I asked if they had ever felt pressured to have sex, while the question about rape came later in the interview. Respecting the definitions that women themselves used meant that it was possible to explore whether and how women come to name and define abuse as particular forms of sexual violence (Kelly, forthcoming). It also necessitated extending the range of terms already in common usage as well as creating new categories – for example, 'coercive sex' for forced sex women described as 'like rape' and 'pressurized sex' to cover situations in which women felt they did not freely choose to have sex.

The forms of child sexual abuse women recalled included assaults which as adults they defined as rape, sexual assault, sexual harassment, flashing, coercive sex and pressurized sex, as well as instances of incestuous abuse. The use of the word 'recalled' is an intentional qualifier, since a number of women remembered some incidents of sexual abuse only between the initial and the follow-up interviews. Many more discussed periods of time when they had forgotten a variety of forms of sexual violence which they had experienced. An awareness that many women may use forgetting as a coping strategy should make us even more cautious of incidence findings and figures. When I analysed the incidence of child sexual abuse in the lives of the women I interviewed, I included all incidents which women experienced as abusive before they were sixteen. Eighty-nine per cent of the women recalled at least one such incident, which is substantially higher than one in four. Moreover, almost two-thirds of this group had experienced two or more forms of sexual abuse.

Exclusion strategies

Many of the current definitions of child sexual abuse – and some of those used by feminists are no exception – specify that it is abuse by an adult of a child. The implicit argument is similar to that used when defining sexual harassment at work in terms of authority relations. In both cases the behaviour of peers is removed from the discussion. Thus child sexual abuse by brothers, cousins, boyfriends, friends, acquaintances and strangers who are close in age to the girl or young woman disappears; all the experiences recounted below, for example, would be excluded:

> I must have been about seven and I was rock climbing with my sister. She was quite far ahead of me and two boys who weren't much older, although they seemed to be to me, came up. One of them held a knife at me and I stood against this rock, they had a good feel around me and then sent me on my way . . . I was just very aware that I shouldn't do anything to aggravate them.

> When I was about seven a twelve-year-old boy terrorized me . . . First it was pull up your dress, and I knew what he was going to say next so I wouldn't. It was like a battle of wills for about fifteen minutes and I was absolutely terrified. In the end I just made a *dash* for it to the next-door neighbours. I found out he'd also done it to my sister. We lived in fear when we came out of school, always looking to make sure he wasn't around.

> Once while I was still at school someone I was going out with attempted to rape me in my own bedroom – I threw him out of the house.

> There was one occasion – it didn't actually get to intercourse purely because the guy had a plaster cast on his leg (laughs), but it was attempted rape. It was a boy I had been going out with – he tried to have intercourse with me over a table – my blouse was ripped. I remember being very frightened . . . I mean I got away from him purely because he had a cast on his leg.

The forms of child sexual abuse by peers recalled by women I interviewed ranged from touching assaults by relatively young boys, through pressurized and coercive sex, to attempted rape and rape by adolescent strangers, acquaintances and boyfriends. Two women were incestuously abused by peers. Recent research in the United Kingdom has also highlighted specific forms of sexual harassment which girls experience at school (Mahony, 1985), and research in the United States has documented the incidence of sexual assault of girls by adolescent boys (Ageton, 1983).

One of the arguments that has graced the *Guardian* letters page over the last month suggests that concern about child sexual abuse is an overreaction, on the grounds that single incidents and 'minor' forms have little impact. One correspondent even went so far as to remove them from discussion altogether by re-analysing incidence figures. Flashing is often used as the example of a 'minor' offence. The majority of incidents of flashing recalled by the women I interviewed occurred before they were sixteen; it is a form of sexual violence that is disproportionately directed at girls and young women. Even though some of them, at the time, did not fully understand what was happening they all remembered feeling threatened and distressed. The women speaking below show that for many women flashing is not 'minor' and that incidents of other forms of child sexual abuse, even if single, can have profound and long-term consequences.

My sister and I used to take the dog for a walk in the park – I didn't understand it at the time but this guy was exposing himself. I've got very dim memories but I do remember it was terrible.

I was about twelve and I was in the park, wheeling my baby sister in her pram – I was very short-sighted (laughs) and this man came along and started talking to me – did I know where babies come from? It wasn't until he was quite near that I realized he was flashing me – it was *awful*, really frightening and upsetting. I didn't tell anyone or talk about it, I just went home and brooded about it.

I've just remembered an experience when I was twelve which really disturbed me for about two years, it was only in my twenties that I could even talk about it. I was molested on the underground . . . this man was sitting opposite with a camera and just started being friendly and talking to me. Me being a nice, friendly, polite child responded. The outcome was, he made me feel him up. Looking back it wasn't that bad, but to me it was the most awful thing that ever happened to me. I've had this repulsion for ever after for soft squiggy moist skin – it would remind me of what I felt. I told my parents and they were very good. I always thought, I'll never get married now, that's put me off men.

When I was twelve or thirteen I used to shoplift . . . One day I got caught by this bloke – I was very naive – who asked if I would deliver a parcel with him. He said I wasn't the usual kind of girl who shoplifted (ironic laugh). I agreed to go with him if he didn't say anything about the shoplifting. Anyway I went to this empty house, went upstairs and he got me to lie on the floor and he did too and was moving backwards and forwards – I presume he was masturbating. At this point I began to get worried and said so and he let me go – which is amazing. I did feel really *awful* afterwards plus there was the feeling that I'd failed my parents . . . I remember thinking when I got home that I was really *unclean*, I washed, *tore* off my clothes. I felt really degraded by it – I felt a lot of the things that women who've been raped feel.

This last woman's recollection of the impact of this experience on her highlights the dramatic effects that single incidents of abuse can have: she was unable to go out shopping for a year afterwards, stopped going out with her friends in case they walked past the house where the assault happened, and did not go out with a man until she went to university.

Inclusion strategies

Taking as a starting point what women and girls define as abusive highlights forms of child sexual abuse which are seldom tapped by questionnaire surveys. One which emerged during the interviews was a form of verbal sexual harassment specific to adolescent girls, a form practised by relatives and strangers, peers and adults. Each woman who talked about it remembered the acute humiliation and embarrassment she felt at the time.

> You'd be walking down the street and groups of blokes would make comments about being 'well developed'.

> I was rather well developed from the age of about thirteen, fourteen onwards and I can remember being pissed off at comments and things.

> It was when my breasts started growing and lots of my male relatives just would make comments about it in front of everyone else – it was really embarrassing. When I blushed they'd laugh and make another comment about that!

That fathers also made these kinds of remarks, coupled with the fact that many women discussed other aspects of their father's behaviour which made them feel uncomfortable and/or confused, raises the question of how we define incestuous abuse and whether we really want to exclude the following:

> It was feelings and it was also things that he did which I was unsure about, which I knew were sexual in some way but . . . like kissing me on the mouth and the way he hugged me.

> I knew there was something funny – I used to hate being alone with him. When I was fifteen he said he loved me and I said 'I know'. He said, 'No, more than that, like I love your mum'. I said, 'Don't be silly, you're my dad!'. He said, 'I'm married to your mum but I'm not your dad'. He used to ask me to have sex with him then.

For the thirteen women who defined their experiences as incest there was also a *range* of experience. For two women the abuse was limited to single incidents of rape; the other eleven women discussed varied patterns of abuse, from fondling and masturbation to eventual rape (six women). Most of the abusers were biological or social fathers, but other abusers included a grandfather, a cousin who was treated as a brother and, in one woman's case, a number of cousins and uncles who lived in the household. What makes incestuous abuse different from other forms of child sexual abuse is that the abuser lives in, and is treated as, a member of the household or family. This gives him both easier and continual sexual access to the girl, as well as other forms of control over her.

The woman speaking below graphically illustrates the problems of defining 'incest' when the point of reference is not the experience of the individual who is being abused but a legal or 'commonsense' definition. Her father was a lawyer and made sure he never did anything which would legally be defined as abuse.

> It remained quite static . . . it consisted of him coming into my room when I was asleep and sitting on the side of my bed and beginning to touch me, which would wake me up. If I was lying on my back or my side I would still pretend to be asleep and would roll over on my stomach so that he couldn't touch my breasts or vagina. He would rub my back and he obviously was sexually excited (sigh) and would tell me I was beautiful . . . [He would] say the same thing over and over again.

During the interview she discussed how difficult it had been for her to define this as incest, despite the enormous impact it had had on her life.

A feminist definition

If we are to reflect in our definition of child sexual abuse the range and complexity of what women and girls experience as abusive we must listen to what they have to say. Some of the experiences recorded here, many others recorded in the interviews and countless others experienced in women's lives would be excluded by the definitions of child sexual abuse which currently inform professional practice and even by some of those used by feminists.

One possible strategy for developing a feminist definition would be to apply the whole range of terms that we already use in relation to abuse of adult women to the abuse of children – for example, flashing, rape, sexual harassment (physical, verbal and visual) and sexual assault. It is, however, also essential to retain the specific category of incest to designate child sexual abuse by a member of the household or family. This allows us to foreground the specific context and dynamics of the abuse, in the same way that 'domestic violence' as a category does in the case of adult women.

It is precisely in order to reflect both the complexity and the range of abuse which women and girls experience that I suggest the use of the concept of a continuum – a continuum based on what women and girls experience as abusive which also allows for some of the ambiguities. In the case of child sexual abuse, such a continuum can also take account of the fact that the same type of assault may be committed by a stranger or a relative, an adult or a peer and can be a single or repeated occurrence.

Implications for feminist theory and practice

Implicit in what I have said so far is that sexual abuse of girls is part of the more general phenomenon of sexual violence. Our analysis of the cause of child sexual abuse must therefore draw on an analysis of gender. It is by making gender the centre of our analysis that abuse by peers can both be taken account of and be accounted for. Abuse by adult men involves the combination of gender power and adult authority, a combination even further amplified when the adult is the girl's father.

When thinking about services for sexually abused girls, as well as prevention programmes in schools, we must reflect the range of forms of abuse that are currently experienced. Taking prevention programmes as an example, a whole range of issues and questions arise in the light of the previous discussion. For example, is abuse by peers taken into account – both in relation to alerting children to the possibility and in relation to working with boys as potential abusers? Do the ways in which child sexual abuse is currently represented in terms of the child's body exclude certain forms of abuse (for example, talking about 'private parts' precludes oral sex, passionate kissing)? Are the protection strategies discussed relevant to all forms of sexual abuse or only some of them? Might telling children to 'just say no' silence those who are resisting but unable to stop abuse, as well as those who feel it is unsafe to resist? These examples demonstrate just how important it is to take full account of the complexity and range of abuse in the case of child sexual abuse.

As feminists we should be taking the same care, asking the same questions, reflecting the same complexity in our theory, research and service work around child sexual abuse as we have been doing in the case of sexual violence against women.

Notes

Liz Kelly is a radical feminist sociologist. She has been a member of her local refuge group and active in Women's Aid since 1974, is a founder member of Norwich Rape Crisis and Norwich Consultants on Sexual Violence and a member of Trouble and Strife Collective. She has recently been appointed research fellow for the Child Abuse Study Unit at the Polytechnic of North London.

References

AGETON, Suzanne, (1983) *Sexual Assault Among Adolescents* Lexington: Lexington Books.

BOGRAD, Michele and YLLO, Kersti (forthcoming) *Feminist Perspectives on Wife Abuse* Beverley Hills: Sage.

FINKELHOR, David (1979) *Sexually Victimized Children* New York: Free Press.

HALL, Ruth (1985) *Ask Any Woman: A London Inquiry into Rape and Sexual Assault* Bristol; Falling Wall Press.

HANMER, Jalna and MAYNARD, Mary (1987) *Women, Violence and Social Control* London: Macmillan.

KELLY, Liz (1986) 'Women's Experiences of Sexual Violence', PhD thesis, Essex University.

KELLY, Liz (1987) 'The Continuum of Sexual Violence' in HANMER and MAYNARD (1987).

KELLY, Liz (forthcoming) 'How Women Define Sexual Violence' in BOGRAD and YLLO (forthcoming).

KELLY, Liz (forthcoming) *Surviving Sexual Violence* Cambridge: Polity Press.

LONDON RAPE CRISIS CENTRE (1987) *Strength in Numbers* London Rape Crisis Centre.

MAHONY, Pat (1985) *Schools for the Boys? Co-education Reassessed* London: Hutchinson.

RUSSELL, Diana (1984) *Sexual Exploitation* Beverley Hills: Sage.

WEST, D. J. (1985) *Sexual Victimization: Two Recent Researches into Sex Problems and Their Social Effects* Aldershot: Gower.

WISE, Sue and STANLEY, Liz (1987) *Georgie Porgie: Sexual Harassment in Everyday Life* London: Pandora Press.

A CASE

Anonymous

Being as I were, an infant, you could say that I were far too young for
fully comprehending what it was I found my father doing to me with his
fingers, under my blanket, between my legs. I have very vivid memories
of being a tiny baby and all I'm able to muster from this particular age is
for everything he were doing to me and for what he made me touch, it
was all very painful. By the time I turned the age of four, I found myself
trying to outsmart my father, with his antics still continuing, only more
regularly. I understood fully the meaning of pain and I often wondered
why he wouldn't kill me or why he chose to inflict such pain upon me. My
father became a very different man when in the company of friends or
relatives, treating his family with sudden happiness and great pride. I
later fully understood the meaning of lies. By the time I was six my
father, in a sense, began to try and replace what he had taken from me
with materialistic values and pouring over me such substances as toys,
etc. I found then it were too late, I was hardly a child any longer. I
reached for everything and had a habit of watching other fathers with
their children. I learned through this 'spying' there was something else.
More than this. I found no need for my father's gifts. My idea of playing
by then was reading up on the reality of the world through the
newspaper, piano playing, drawing naked pictures in crayon of people I
knew (school teachers I despised, etc.), telling the time repeatedly to my
mum and to anyone that would listen and, by the time I was nine,
writing poetry (not to exclude alcohol and drugs as part of a regular diet
by the age of twelve). I had tendencies to throw toys into the street, up
against the concrete walls in the cellar, etc. I was happy ruining
everything my father ever gave me. I looked at money and objects which
it could purchase as being cold. Money and materialistic values has
become a well-theorized fixture in my mind as being cold, and still exists
to this day.

Feminist Review No 28, January 1988

By the age of ten I was certain I had discovered better ways and through my discoveries I found myself searching something better for myself, someplace else in the world. Far, far away from my house and the helpful advice, better known as widely spread myths, that my father had registered into his children. I remember crying myself to sleep and begging GOD to help me get out. Once, my father caught me doing this. I think it was then he had realized that I knew very well the difference of good from bad and that he was very bad. He didn't like the idea that all he had taught me, with his threats and years of intimidation, were no longer working. He finally felt threatened by me and this became evident shortly before everything had surfaced.

My father owned a .22 calibre shotgun and he threatened both my sister and myself by placing the gun to the side of our heads and swearing to take our lives. Anything, I believe, is survivable as long as you are able to think quickly and carefully calculate the right words to say, in correct text, to a fallen pervert with a gun in hand. He never pulled the trigger.

My father taught me how to shoot this gun and I became very good. I myself contemplated killing my father with his own gun. Back in 1977, November sometime, I found myself guilty, pacing the cellar floor sometime past midnight, staring up through the beams on the ceiling where the gun and some bullets were kept. I was fully clothed and ready to run. 'Catch me if you can!' I began to think, as I often do, quite fairly, 'Pity this man'. I didn't want to give in to his ways. Ridding his faults by ridding his victims. I went back up to my bedroom and fell asleep. I never touched the gun again.

In the autumn of 1978 my sister phoned my mum from her school. She asked my mum if she would come to get her because she had a great secret that she could no longer keep quiet. I give my sister a lot of credit for doing this. My mum had frequented as a patient to a psychiatric ward since I was four. No, my mum wasn't aware of what was happening to her daughters. When my sister told her of the things my father had done to her and for how long he was commiting such acts, she believed her and asked my sister a simple question. She asked my sister if she were all right. My mum has always had a great belief in her children and she rarely ever scolded us. I was always out to protect my mum, because she was and still is very much like a child, delicate and seemingly untouched. I had always been afraid to tell her, for if she were, say, 'in the wrong frame of mind' GOD only knows what she would have said to my father and GOD only knows how he would have reacted. To me he had frequently threatened her life.

My father did outsmart me in one way. He had verbally antagonized my sister every evening at the dinner table. He called her such names as 'dumb', 'ignorant' and swear to her she was ugly until he succeeded in making her cry. Then, he would point his finger to me, calling me 'the better of the two', or 'the best child'. He made her hate me and I don't blame her. He had successfully separated us, so neither of us grew aware that his sexual 'desires' were happening to the both of us. We grew up in the same house, laughed and cried over similar things, but we never became close enough to talk to each other. We were sisters and my father had made us out to be 'unequal', as two very different people. Neither my sister or myself were good enough for one another. My sister was easily convinced, much like my mum. I was easily fooled, say, like my father was, eventually.

My parents were divorced in 1978.

DEFENDING INNOCENCE:
Ideologies of Childhood

Jenny Kitzinger

Over the last few years there has been a revival of public concern about child sexual abuse. A heterogenous child protection movement has evolved, promoting preventative work in schools and initiating projects such as the children's help line, ChildLine. There has been a major public information campaign, articles about child sex abuse have appeared in most women's magazines and there have been several TV documentaries. Central to all these branches of the campaign is the challenging of various miconceptions about child sex abuse: misconceptions about the nature and frequency of the abuse, the type of perpetrator and the role of the family (Adams and Fay, 1981; Justice and Justice, 1979). The movement seeks to replace old 'myths' with new 'facts'. The myth/fact scenario, however, serves to obscure the political dimensions of the 'new' approaches to child sexual abuse. Facts do not 'speak for themselves' and there are many questions to be raised about the images of manhood, womanhood, motherhood and family life that are emerging out of the campaigns. Some of these questions have been discussed elsewhere (Kitzinger, 1988), but here I want to focus on the images of childhood promoted in the public education programmes and the reporting of child sexual abuse in the media.

Most of us are now familiar with the images of childhood associated with discussions of child sexual abuse on TV, in newspapers and in child protection leaflets. The abused child is represented by an anonymous figure sitting limp and despairing with her head in her hands, or by the brother and sister gazing out wistfully from behind a window, or, sometimes, simply by a broken doll. These images can be objectifying and voyeuristic in themselves but, however 'tasteful', they invariably emphasize the child's youth and passivity.

When particular cases are documented, the pen-portraits of the victim always focus on child-specific attributes such as pigtails, hair-

ribbons, her sailor-suit dress, her 'favourite plastic purse with the rainbow handles' or her Paddington Bear clock (*Sun*, 10.12.86; *Mirror*, 9.12.86; *Today*, 2.6.87). Even 'serious investigative journalism' documenting children's sexual exploitation may employ, as background music, the tinkling sound of a musical box (e.g. Cook, 1987). All these props accentuate the fact that the victim is a child – childhood itself is an issue; in case we are in any doubt, the sexual abuse of a child is often referred to as 'the theft or violation of childhood' (Barr, 1986; *Sun*, 13.12.86; Bradbury, 1986).

Implicit, then, in all such documentation is an assertion of what childhood 'really is'. Childhood is presented as a time of play, an asexual and peaceful existence within the protective bosom of the family. This image is both ethnocentric and unrealistic. Even while addressing some of the horrors of childhood, these reports confirm myths about the 'true essence of childhood' which contradict the experiences of the majority of young people. Here I want to focus on the child protection movement's emphasis on two particular qualities of 'real' childhood – innocence and vulnerability.

Childhood innocence

The child protection movement is fighting against a long tradition which views the victim of sexual abuse as an active participant and which presents the child victim as a 'Lolita' or 'nymphette' (Nelson, 1987; Rush, 1980). The emphasis on children's innocence in part serves to counteract these negative stereotypes, but it has also become a fetishistic focus in itself. Books about child sexual abuse have titles like: *The Betrayal of Innocence* (Forward and Buck, 1981) or *The Death of Innocence* (Janus, 1981), and 'robbing children of their innocence' has become synonymous with sexual abuse (*Sun*, 13.12.86; *Mirror*, 10.12.86; *Star*, 15.11.86).

Innocence is a powerful and emotive symbol, but to use it to provoke public revulsion against sexual abuse is counterproductive. For a start the notion of childhood innocence is itself a source of titillation for abusers. A glance at pornography leaves little doubt that innocence is a sexual commodity. 'Kiddie porn' magazines specifically set out to highlight the purity of their child models (Rush, 1980: 164). Advertising produces images of young girls made up to look like Marilyn Monroe, with slogans like 'Innocence is sexier than you think' (Rush, 1980: 125), and the fashion industry cashes in with baby-doll nightdresses for adult

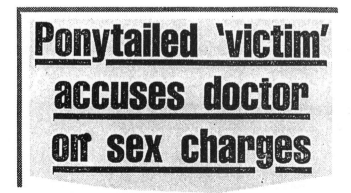

The term 'ponytailed victim', rather like the phrase 'gymslip mum', serves to draw together and exploit the contrast between traditional understandings of childhood on the one hand (as signified by ponytails and gym-slips) and sex and violence on the other. From the Daily Mirror *9 December 1986*

women and T-shirts emblazoned with the words 'Forbidden Fruit' for girls. In a society where innocence is a fetish and where men are excited by the idea of defiling the pure and deflowering the virgin, focusing on children's presumed innocence only reinforces men's desire for them as sexual objects. As one child abuser said, 'It was so exciting, she was so young, so pure and clean' (*Star*, 4.12.86).

Secondly, 'innocence' is a suspect concept to employ in the fight against child sexual abuse because it stigmatizes the 'knowing' child. The romanticism of childhood innocence excludes those who do not conform to the ideal. A precocious child who appears flirtatious and sexually aware may forfeit her claims to protection because, if the violation of innocence is the criterion by which the act of sexual abuse is judged, violating a 'knowing' child is a lesser offence than violating an 'innocent' child.[1] It is this notion which allows abusers to defend themselves on the grounds that their victim was 'no angel'. One abuser, for instance, argued that his victim was no innocent – she drank, smoked and often failed to do her homework. He should know – he was her headmaster (*Daily Mail*, 14.12.85).

The notion of 'innocence' and, therefore, the potential for the loss of innocence can also facilitate further victimization:

> The sexually victimized child may be viewed neither as a child nor as an adult but rather as a piece of 'damaged goods' lacking the attributes of both childhood and adult . . . sexually victimized children may become 'walking invitations'. (Sgroi, 1982: 114).

A child who is known to be a victim of sexual abuse is often subject to further exploitation: 'a bizarre spin-off of the labelling process is the fascination the girl presents to others. . . . Publicly deflowered as she is, she is regarded as no longer deserving respect or protection' (Summit and Kryso, 1978: 244).

Innocence, then, is a problematic concept because it is itself a sexual commodity and because a child who is anything less than 'an angel' may be seen as 'fair game', both by the courts and by other men who will avail themselves of a child they know has previously been abused (Ward, 1984: 159; Sarnacki Porter *et al.*, 1982: 114). More fundamentally, however, 'innocence' should be rejected because it is an ideology used to deny children access to knowledge and power (Jackson, 1982).

In the name of 'childhood innocence' adults repress children's own expressions of sexuality, deny them control over their own bodies and 'protect' them from knowledge. Indeed it is the notion of innocence that stops some parents telling their children about incest (*Independent*, 28.4.87) because they do not want to 'corrupt the few years of innocence that should be every child's right' (Brown, 1986). It also leads to those working to expose child abuse being accused of destroying the 'age of innocence' by highlighting sexual exploitation (*News on Sunday*, 3.5.87).

Protecting the weak

Another theme running through much of the literature on the abuse of children is that of 'protection'. Children, it is pointed out, are weak, but there is little if any analysis of the structural power imbalances which make that so. An analysis of power is rejected in favour of a paternalistic approach. Parents are advised to step up surveillance over their children, and to avoid letting them out alone or at night (*Foster Care*, 1986). They can now even buy 'Toddler Minders', electronic tags rather like those proposed for prisoners under house arrest, which set off an alarm if the child strays outside a certain area (*Observer*, 17.8.86). Such siege mentality puts a huge strain on the mother. It also places children under curfew and encourages children to live in fear:

> What are acceptable limits on a child's freedom? The short walk to the newsagent's? The chip shop? A quarter of a mile? A hundred yards? No further than the front gate? In such a climate is it possible to foster the sense of personal independence that is as important as caution? (Brown, 1986)

There is another problem in that the focus is, yet again, on curtailing the freedom of the potential victims rather than curtailing the freedom of potential abusers. The child protection movement's focus on the victims evades the fact that vulnerability does not exist in a vacuum but only has meaning in relation to something – that is, a threat.

This approach is flawed from a short-term, practical as well as from a long-term and ideological point of view. A curfew on children will not protect them because most abuse happens in the victim's own home, or that of the offender (Finkelhor, 1979: 74). As one incest survivor points out:

> 'I was never afraid, when going home at night, of being raped or mugged, I knew what was waiting for me was infinitely worse'. (Quoted in Cogan and Caplin, 1986)

It is disturbing that many child protectionists persist in presenting the home as a sanctuary and warning children to 'Say No to Strangers' (the title of the Home Office film). Ironically, such advice increases children's isolation and confinement within the family (Barrett and Coward, 1985: 23) and suggests a need for increased parental control (Ennew, 1986: 69).

The call on paternal protection is particularly inappropriate given that the father or stepfather may well be the abuser. The father's role as protector is, on one level, quite compatible with his role as possessor – the notion of ownership lies behind both the duty to protect and the right to use. The father or brother who is assigned to defend a woman's virginity and to 'give her away' in marriage may, by the same token, claim the right to use her sexually himself (Herman, 1981: 54).

'Protection' then is not a long-term (and often not even a short-term) solution to the exploitation of children, and similarly 'vulnerability' is not a useful focus for the debate. Indeed 'vulnerability' is an important ideological barrier against children's liberation and is a concept used to pre-empt discussion about structural oppression. Even some of the pioneers of feminist analyses of child sexual abuse have accepted, and been limited by, this emphasis.[2] Florence Rush, after her radical and detailed analysis of the historical and cultural context of such abuse, states:

> I believe the term liberation as it is carelessly applied to children is both
> dangerous and absurd. Born helpless and vulnerable, the young have
> always relied upon the greater capacity of adults for survival. . . . To
> equate the oppression of children with oppressed blacks and women is to
> confuse the nature of childhood. (Rush, 1980: 186)

She goes on to conclude that: 'Children have the right, not to equality with adults, but to considerate adult understanding, custody and protection' (1980: 186).

I agree with Rush that it is misleading to take the concept of liberation developed by one oppressed group and to transfer it wholesale to another. There are important differences between the oppressions experienced by people because of their stigmatized age and/or race, gender and/or class. However, this is not a reason for rejecting 'liberation' and retreating into some kind of protectionist philosophy. We can struggle to develop a more appropriate analysis of children's oppression instead of compromising into the reductionist position that, because children are 'helpless', they need protection rather than rights.

Oppressed groups have good reason to be suspicious of any theory which relies on biological determinism. There is a long tradition of explaining and excusing oppression on the grounds of biology as if we were confined by nature rather than by a man-made world. In the west, for instance, notions of innate biological weakness have been used to excuse the 'fair sex' (that is, white, middle-class women) from paid work and political power. Weakness is a criterion selectively applied – Black and working-class women have rarely been offered the privileges of protection and even white, middle-class women have forfeited any claims to fragility when they've become too uppity. In a similar way the 'vulnerability' accorded to children as a category is no protection for the child who does not 'fit' or who steps out of line.

It is important not to be seduced by supposedly commonsense interpretation of biological 'limitations' or by the promised offer of protection. Instead I would argue that the notion of children's innate vulnerability (as a biological fact unmediated by the world they live in) is an ideology of control which diverts attention away from the socially constructed oppression of children. As Jackson (1982) points out, children in western society are kept dependent for much longer than is considered necessary in other societies. Young people are politically disenfranchized, economically restricted and denied the legal rights and responsibilities that are considered part of full citizenship. Their dependence is accentuated:

> A great deal of effort is spent in keeping children childish. . . . Children who behave like adults are regarded as at best amusing and at worst thoroughly obnoxious. If we were not so interested in nurturing immaturity, would the word 'precocious' have become an insult? (Jackson, 1982: 27)

This is an area where theories of children's liberation can usefully borrow ideas from other liberation movements which demand rights and resources rather than appealing for pity and protection (women reject chivalry and the offer of seats and demand maternity leave and crèches instead; the physically disabled reject the 'helping hand' in favour of a new architecture).

If we are to tackle the roots of child sexual abuse we have to think about the position of children in society. Perhaps the first step is to change the terms of the debate by replacing the concept of 'vulnerability' with terms such as 'oppression' or 'powerlessness' and by replacing restrictive notions of 'protecting' with liberating notions of 'empowering'.

Adult awareness, children's assertiveness: one step forward

In spite of such criticism, many preventative programmes in specific ways do link child sexual abuse to the broader position of children in society, even if they fail to develop a wider theoretical approach. These child protection programmes challenge the stereotype that children often lie, and question the techniques employed by adults to silence children and bully them into obedience ('Do as you are told', 'Because I say so', 'It's for your own good'). They make connexions between the way we refuse to listen to children generally and the way we fail to hear about abuse:

> 'We are too accustomed to regarding children as an irritation, a noisy messy nuisance. If we continue to believe children should be seen and not heard, their silence protects the molester.' (Paul Griffiths, quoted in Rantzen, 1986)

Many of the new writings draw attention to the ways in which we deny children control over their own bodies, whether by making them kiss Daddy goodnight or by hitting them (Adams and Fay, 1981: 14–15). They challenge us to reassess our own use of power in all areas, not only as parents but as 'strangers', youth workers and teachers. As one headmistress says:

> 'You can't teach children that they are responsible for certain areas of their life and then expect them to sit in a classroom and force-feed them with information they are not encouraged to discuss or query. The compliant, conforming child becomes one who is at risk.' (Linda Frost, quoted in Aziz, 1987).

Such discussion helps us to become aware of the day-to-day way in which we relate to children and to change our own behaviour so that we minimize our collaboration with a social structure that is profoundly anti-children.[3]

Our treatment of children is not, however, simply a question of attitude; it is a reflection of our position of power over children.

> Childhood is not just a psychological state, but also a social status – and a very lowly one at that. Take one example: the frequency with which children are touched by adults. The amount of unsolicited physical contact people receive is a good indication of relative social position. It has been observed that bosses touch workers, men touch women and adults touch children much more than the other way round. To touch one's social superior without good reason is an act of insubordination. Think how frequently children are shaken off when they use touch to attract an adult's attention, and how that same adult can freely take hold of the child, adjust his or her hair, cut short his or her activities. (Jackson, 1982: 26)

Reconsidering our treatment of children is an important part of challenging the lowly social status of children, but it does not, in itself, solve the inequalities.

The preventative programmes are also trying to encourage children to change their behaviour. They are being encouraged to be assertive ('It's OK to say NO') to get in touch with and express their own feelings ('Feeling Yes, Feeling No') and to develop a sense of control over their own bodies. This is the positive side of the action taken in response to the ideology of vulnerability – here vulnerability is seen not just in terms of the need for adult protection but as something that children themselves can change by modifying their behaviour. Roleplays, games, stories and songs are being specifically designed to help children resist abuse. The message is, as one catchy song declares:

> My body's nobody's body but mine
> You mind your own body
> Let me mind mine. (*Kids Can Say No* video)

Such promotion of children's 'rights' is, however, cosmetic in so far as children are still supposed to obey legitimate authority. The preventative campaigns aim to increase children's self-confidence but adults are reassured that 'teaching children to say ño' is not 'subversive' (Aziz, 1987). It 'doesn't mean they are going to say no to drinking milk or eating greens just for the hell of it' (Linda Frost quoted in Aziz, 1987). In other words, the child protection movement encourages children to express their opinions but in the end expects them to do what is 'for their own good' as defined by benevolent adults who make 'reasonable' requests.

Such isolated assertiveness training is hardly radical and, in any case, is unlikely to have much long-term effect. Even if a child is told that 'bodily autonomy' is her right, she is likely to be getting a different implicit message every day. 'My body', maybe *should* be 'nobody's body but mine' but children are subject to daily bodily invasion: they are not only raped and molested but their bodies are subject to laws which they are powerless to influence, their images are exploited in advertising, and adults control what they wear, what they can do and when they can do it. A child cannot develop some kind of abstract concept of bodily autonomy without any practical experience of that 'right':

> A child's right to her own body, autonomy and privacy is still a radical concept which would require the transformation of family power relations. (Liz, 1982: 217)

Assertiveness training is a start but it is not a solution and it is certainly a misnomer to call it a 'preventative' measure; training individuals to be assertive without challenging practical inequalities is no more 'preventative' of child sexual abuse than building nuclear bunkers is 'preventative' of nuclear war.

Child protection programmes which focus on helping children to change their attitudes in isolation are at best providing individualistic solutions. At worst they are creating the illusion that victims have powers to resist that in reality are negligible. While it is important that children are not terrorized into feeling they have no ability to protect themselves (and in some situations they will indeed be able to fight off an attacker), it is vital to recognize that a child can confidently shout 'No' at her father and still find that he rapes her because in the end it is he who has the power. The message that children can protect themselves if they are assertive can be misleading. It can also reinforce children's sense of guilt by making then feel somehow responsible for what has happened because maybe they did not say 'no' as though they *really* meant it.

To sum up, despite some encouraging individual aspects of the contemporary child protection movement, the mainstream campaigns conspicuously fail to take any overall stand against the structural oppression of children. They are, therefore, not only severely limited in what they can achieve, but they also often reinforce the very ideologies which expose children to exploitation in the first place.

Notes

Jenny Kitzinger was involved in setting up CHOICES, the Cambridge Incest Survivors Refuge where she has worked for the last three years as a volunteer counsellor and Jane-of-all-trades. Her paid work is at the Child Care and Development Group, University of Cambridge.

I am just starting work on a book about childhood sexual abuse and would like to interview women who have experienced childhood sexual abuse or whose children have been abused and/or who work in this field. If you would be prepared to fill in a questionnaire or be interviewed, please write to me at: CC & D, Free School Lane, Cambridge, CB2 3RF. Thank you.

1 The same notion of the deserving and undeserving victim has of course been used about adult rape victims. When Peter Sutcliffe raped and murdered women in Yorkshire, more concern was shown about his 'innocent' victims than about the prostitutes he attacked.
2 The mainstream child protection movement as discussed in this chapter is a set of ideas rather than a group of individuals. Some of the people quoted do not necessarily see themselves as 'mainstream' and indeed may also express quite revolutionary views. Some writers, such as Rush, discuss child abuse in terms of power and social structure and yet make statements which undermine more radical accounts, or, at the very least, lend themselves to liberal co-option. It is precisely these contradictions and the pervasiveness of mainstream thought (or the co-option of radical ideas) that make detailed analysis of these constructs so important.
3 In spite of women's direct personal experience of the oppressions of childhood, the feminist movement seems to have generally evaded this issue. Women's movement texts tend to discuss children only in relation to women (as sources of joy or sorrow, fulfilment or entrapment) or as objects of sexist conditioning. Out of the 175 references to children in *The Feminist Dictionary* (Kramarae and Treichler, 1985) and *The Quotable Woman* (Partnow, 1985) less than a dozen deal with children's social status.

References

ADAMS, C and FAY, J. (1981) *No More Secrets: Protecting Your Child from Sexual Assault* California: Impact Publishers.

AZIZ, C. (1987) 'Teaching Children to Say No' *Guardian*, 6 January, pp. 10.

BARR, A. (1986) 'Child Sex Abuse: We Need Money Not Sentiment' *Observer*, weekend 9 November, p. 51.

BARRETT, M. and COWARD, R. (1985) 'Don't Talk to Strangers' *New Socialist*, November 1985, pp. 21–3.

BRADBURY, A. (1986) 'A Model of Treatment' *Community Care*, 4 September, pp. 24–5.

BROWN, M. (1986) 'A Parent's Dilemma' *Sunday Times*, 19 October.

COGAN, R. and CAPLIN, S. (1986) 'Child Abuse: A New Initiative' *Observer*, 26 October.

COOK, R. (1987) *The Cook Report*, ITV, 8.30 p.m. 29 July.

ENNEW, J. (1986) *The Sexual Exploitation of Children*, Cambridge: Polity Press.

FINKELHOR, D. (1979) *Sexually Victimized Children* London: Macmillan.

FORWARD, S. and BUCK, C. (1981) *Betrayal of Innocence: Incest and its Devastation* Harmondsworth: Penguin.

FOSTER CARE (1986) 'Streetproof Your Children', June, p. 29.

HERMAN, J. (1981) *Father–Daughter Incest*, Cambridge, Mass: Harvard University Press.

HOLLY, L. (1988) editor *The Sexual Agenda of Schooling* Milton Keynes: Open University Press (forthcoming).

HOWARD LEAGUE WORKING PARTY (1985) *Unlawful Sex* London: Waterloo Publishers.

JACKSON, S. (1982) *Childhood and Sexuality* Oxford: Blackwells.

JANUS, S. (1981) *The Death of Innocence* New York: Morrow.

JUSTICE, B. and JUSTICE, R. (1979) *The Broken Taboo* London: Peter Owen.

KIDS CAN SAY NO video, Pergamon Educational Productions, Exeter.

KITZINGER, J. (1987) 'The Sexual Abuse of Children' *Values* Vol. 2, no. 1.

KITZINGER, J. (1988) 'The Politics of the Child Protection Movement' in HOLLY (1988).

KRAMARAE, C. and TREICHLER, P. (1985) *A Feminist Dictionary* London: Pandora Press.

LIZ (1982) 'Too Afraid to Speak' *The Leveller*, 12–15 April, pp. 18–21.

LONDON RAPE CRISIS CENTRE (1984) *Sexual Violence, The Reality for Women* London: The Women's Press.

NELSON, S. (1987) *Incest: Fact and Myth* Edinburgh: Stramullion Press.

PARTNOW, E. (1985) *The Quotable Woman* New York: Facts on File.

RANTZEN, E. (1986) 'Dear Esther' *Sunday Times* 9 November, p. 25.

RUSH, F. (1980) *The Best Kept Secret: Sexual Abuse of Children* New York: McGraw-Hill.

SARNACKI PORTER, F., CANFIELD BLICK, L. and SGROI, S. (1982) 'Treatment of the Sexually Abused Child' in SGROI (1982).

SGROI, S. (1982) editor *Handbook of Clinical Intervention in Child Sexual Abuse* Cambridge, Mass: Lexington Books.

SUMMIT, R. and KRYSO, J. (1978) 'Sexual Abuse of Children: A Clinical Spectrum' *American Journal of Orthopsychiatry* 48, pp. 237–51.

WARD, E. (1984) *Father–Daughter Rape* London: The Women's Press.

FEMINISM AND THE SEDUCTIVENESS OF THE 'REAL EVENT'

Ann Scott

Some ten or fifteen years ago, when feminists began thinking seriously about psychoanalysis, the most common expression of doubt was: but isn't Freud culturally specific? Weren't the illness and disturbance he described true for the period, but times have changed? Today we have the appearance of a reversal: now that the extent of child sexual abuse is increasingly recognized, some people are asking the other side of the question: if Freud was so mistaken about the reality of the 'real event', does psychoanalysis have any credibility at all? In one sense nothing has changed: there will probably always be rational and irrational forms of ambivalence, not to say scepticism, about the validity of Freud's theory of the mind and its motives. However, in this article I want to look at the implications for psychoanalysis, and the varieties of feminist response to psychoanalysis, of these specifically new terms of discussion. For there is no doubt that the current, unprecedented concern with the reality of child abuse must lead one to look again at the methodological implications of Freud's work during the period which resulted in his writing, of the women patients who spoke of having been seduced as girls by their fathers, 'I no longer believe in my *neurotica*' (Freud to Wilhelm Fliess, 21 September 1897, quoted in Clark 1980: 161).

There has always been a debate inside psychoanalysis about the status of 'real' and 'fantasy', but nothing compares, for events in the public domain, with the recent furore over Freud's seduction theory, and I'll begin by sketching the facts of the Malcolm–Masson controversy. In December 1983 the *New Yorker* ran a two-part article by Janet Malcolm, author of *Psychoanalysis: The Impossible Profession*. 'Trouble in the Archives' went over, in Malcolm's elegant and intelligent way, a sequence of events between 1974 and 1981 with three main protagonists: Kurt Eissler, a senior New York analyst and secretary of the Sigmund Freud Archives, established in the 1950s to secure a collection of posthumous and Freud-related material; Anna Freud, then working in London and living in the Freud family home in Maresfield Gardens that was to become the Freud Museum after her death; and Jeffrey Moussaieff Masson, a young Canadian Sanskritist who had trained as a psychoanalyst and was being groomed to succeed Eissler at the Archives.

While researching the origins of psychoanalysis in Freud's personal papers at Anna Freud's home, Masson came across discrepancies between the original and published versions of correspondence which led him to the conclusion that Freud had suppressed his knowledge of the extent of childhood seduction. When Freud abandoned the seduction theory, Masson argued, he was acting in bad faith and did so in order to protect his standing as a respectable member of the scientific community. The ensuing conflict between Masson, on the one hand, who went public in articles in the *New York Times*, and Eissler and Anna Freud, on the other, resulted in Masson's being sacked as projects director of the Archives, in an atmosphere of raw and unbearably intense feeling.

'Trouble in the Archives' raised a storm of interest at the time and later appeared in book form. Meanwhile, Masson had published *The Assault on Truth: Freud's Suppression of the Seduction Theory*. There his view, briefly, is that Freud's understanding of hysteria, up to and including the 1896 paper 'The Aetiology of Hysteria', was important and compassionate. Masson (1984b: 36) cites Freud's cry, 'Poor child, what have they done to you?', as an example of this work. When Freud 'abandoned' the seduction theory, however, he did a disservice to psychoanalysis with which all subsequent analysts have colluded. Psychoanalysis, as a theory and clinical practice, has denied the reality of sexual abuse, and in so doing has sentenced thousands of patients to confused, guilty silence while exonerating the abusers.

The chronology is complex, fastidious even, as is often the case with such public rows. In the introduction to one of the later editions of his book, Masson states that the individualistic focus of Malcolm's articles obscured the more substantial issues of psychoanalytic theory that he had tried to raise in the book. Then shortly after his book came out, *Mother Jones*, the American radical monthly, gave Masson the opportunity to argue his case. Here he concentrated on two issues. One was the disillusionment he experienced as an analytic trainee in North America: an embarrassing intellectual level, an exaggerated reverence for Freud, etc. (He is not the first to venture such observations.) The other was the similarity he believed he had uncovered between how *his* discoveries were misbelieved and denied by the analytic establishment, and how women's reality is denied. In this way he linked his work on sexual abuse with the feminist issue of male supremacy most directly. Moreover, many of Masson's warmest acknowledgements (1984a, xx; 1984b) go to the 'speaking bitterness' women's literature of recent years – autobiographical testimony, empirical data on abuse, campaigning writing – which serious feminists do take seriously.

What should we make of this constellation of views, ideological positions and hurt feelings? Let me start by attending to the character of these two sets of writing. Malcolm's articles fizz along, sophisticated in the best *New Yorker* way, sharp, observant, framed by the usual gloomily understated cartoons. Malcolm has her detractors, though I am not among them. 'Trouble in the Archives' succeeds well in documenting the appalling personal suffering experienced by all concerned – the slew of idealizations, careerism, insults, disappointment, ostracism among any group of people falling out – without trivializing the issues (though the deeper merits of the issues, in scholarly terms, are not her topic). Masson's book and *Mother Jones* article, by contrast, have an alternately bludgeoning, now self-justifying tone, despite the significance of the issues that he raises and the evidence he adduces in their support. Permeating the whole book is a quality of muddling, muddled thought – with confusions of logic, mistakes of fact, caricatures of others' positions – all of which of necessity weakens the force of his argument. For Masson would have been on to something important, if he had been right. It is a tautology, but worth setting down. If Masson's accusations had been true, then the psychoanalytic community would justly have been on the defensive.

I shall quote a typical passage from his book, to give the reader the feel of his thought, but before going any further it is worth making the general point, as many have done, that it is what Freud put in place of the seduction theory – the theory of infantile sexuality, which attributes unconscious drives and desires to infants and children – which got him into much greater difficulty with the orthodoxy, professional and intellectual, than the seduction theory had ever done. It was because Freud either had to abandon his work when he came to doubt that actual seduction was a necessary precursor of neurotic illness, 'or realize that what he had been doing was only a beginning: respecting what his patients said really did matter in a way he could not have appreciated before' (Parsons 1986: 476), that he was able to work out the distinction between historical and psychical truth which informs all thinking about fantasy as a structure.

To return to *The Assault on Truth*. Taking up Freud's 1916 view (in the *Introductory Lectures*) that stories of childhood seduction in which the father figures regularly as the seducer involve 'an imaginary . . . accusation', and that (in Freud's words) 'up to the present we have not succeeded in pointing to any difference in the consequences, whether phantasy or reality has had the greater share in these events of childhood', Masson writes:

> But in actuality there is an essential difference between the effects of an act that took place and one that was imagined.
> To tell someone who has suffered the effects of a childhood filled with sexual violence that it does not matter whether his memories are anchored in reality or not is to do further violence to that person and is bound to have a pernicious effect. A real memory demands some form of

validation from the outside world – denial of those memories can lead to a break with reality, and a psychosis . . .

. . . in fact psychoanalysts have always shown a greater interest in the fantasy life of a patient than in real events. Freud shifted the interest of psychoanalysis to the pathogenic effects of fantasies, putting less emphasis on the pathogenic effects of real memories in repression. The ideal analytic patient has come to be a person without serious trauma in his childhood. (1984a: 133)

One of the most obvious criticisms of this way of thinking is that it leaves no room for the possibility that Freud could make an error of judgement, perhaps a grave one – in this case about the after-effects of a real seduction – without this compromising the whole fabric of psychoanalytic thought and its development by subsequent generations of analysts. It is noticeable that Masson's overriding interest is in probing the motives for Freud's alleged disingenuousness (my words, not Masson's; see also Krüll, 1979, for a similar concern with Freud's personal motives for dropping the seduction theory), rather than exploring what becomes of key aspects of psychoanalytic theory if the nature of the real event and its consequences is being reconsidered. I am thinking of the concepts of repression, transference, unconscious conflict, secondary gain in illness, repetition compulsion, working through, projection, projective identification, and so forth. For Masson does not address the issue of how much or how little, at the level of mental structure, depends on the reality or fantasy of a special kind of experience.

Another observation. Psychoanalysis is often criticized on 'genetic' grounds, that is, for inappropriately treating an account of the origins of something as an adequate form of explanation of it. Masson, ironically, is constructing a genetic type of argument, for he writes as though everything of significance about psychoanalysis takes the form of an original betrayal. It is a confusion at two levels. Between internal and external, in the first place, for in one sense Masson is right to say that 'psychoanalysts have always shown a greater interest in the fantasy life of a patient than in real events' – but only in the sense that psychoanalysts cannot assume that an (external) event bears within it an unalterable (internal) meaning. It is this confusion, too, which allows Masson to draw his caricature of a conclusion: 'the ideal analytic patient has come to be a person without serious traumas in his childhood', because he is mistakenly ascribing to psychoanalysis the view that it is *only* fantasy which has an impact or an effect: indeed that there is no relationship between fantasy and event. In psychoanalysis, however, all events *become* invested with fantasy, conscious and unconscious, and may on occasion be potentiated *by* fantasy.

In the second place, Masson confusingly identifies 'real memory' solely with 'the event' – as though people have real memories only of their status as object for the other. 'Real memories' can be of thoughts, too, and thought may sometimes take the form of fantasy, and fantasy is unconscious. Such thought demands its own validation: thus for many

The covers of Jeffrey Masson's and Alice Miller's books are representations of violence in which the body – male and female – is fragmented. The expression on the women's faces photographed for the cover of The Assault on Truth *is a mix of desire and sorrow, while* Thou Shalt Not Be Aware *reproduces an extract from Rembrandt's 'Abraham and Isaac'. Freud haunts Masson on the* Mother Jones *cover.*

people in analysis, it is the very complexity, indeed inaccessibility of their own 'personal store of memories' (to borrow a phrase of Masson's), with its interweaving of accuracy and distortion, which is at the centre of the analytic process. Of recent work Ronald Fraser's *In Search of a Past* (1984) is probably the most convincing and haunting recon-struction of such a process of mapping. Fraser explored his own childhood and the memories of the servants he had known as a child, combining the practices of psychoanalysis and oral history, in the attempt to come to terms with his deep sense of having been split as a child. It is just such a 'deep sense' (1984: 106–7) which structures his reality, and forms the strongest possible contrast with Masson's notion of the event as the real.

Put simply, I believe *The Assault on Truth* is misdescribing the place psychoanalysis attributes to real events, whether in general or in the specific form of sexual abuse. I will return to this in the wider context of the analytic community's response to Masson's work. Here I will note the interestingly similar trajectory in the writing of the Swiss psycho-analyst Alice Miller, although one of the significant differences between Miller and Masson is that Miller practised clinically for more than twenty years before giving up this work to write and campaign about child abuse. (Masson acknowledges Miller's influence on his work, and says he owes her 'a great deal' – Malcolm 1984: 14.) In their original German editions, only two years separate her first three books, *The Drama of the Gifted Child, For Your Own Good*, and *Thou Shalt Not Be Aware*. That period charts Miller's explosive turning away from her enlightened but orthodox psychoanalytic view of disturbances, within and between people, to her current, fiercely polemical work on parental power over children (*For Your Own Good* and *Thou Shalt Not Be Aware*), with its combination of hostility and respect for Freudian thought. *The Drama of the Gifted Child* is not just different in rhetoric, but conceptually very far from the two more recent works. *Drama*, still embedded in the psychoanalytic, and widely influential within that world, is a delicate, Winnicottian exploration of the way in which the mother–child relationship, often in the case of gifted, sensitive children, can fail the child because the mother is herself narcissistically deprived.

The originality of Miller's thesis was two-fold. She first separated the analytic notion of narcissism from its pejorative connotation, positing a child's narcissistic needs as authentic, and distinguishing between intellectual development – which could survive maternal failure – and emotional development – which could not, for the mother would be using the child to meet her own unmet needs. Next, and more radically, she compared this relationship with the analyst–analysand relation, suggesting that analysts too could use patients for their own narcissistic purposes. I have drawn this out in order to illustrate the point that Miller's initial stance took up the problem of parental failure in a wide-ranging way – implying, in so many words, that destructiveness, intrusiveness and failure to observe boundaries (all key terms in the literature of sexual abuse) could take a number of forms, many of a subtly interactive kind.

For Your Own Good and *Thou Shalt Not Be Aware* are both more ambitious works. *For Your Own Good* chronicles eighteenth- and nineteenth-century German approaches to child-rearing in an attempt at explaining social cruelty and sadism on the basis that what was done to children is what these children, as adults and parents, later do to others. *Thou Shalt Not Be Aware* is a sustained polemic against all forces in society – ideological, psychiatric, psychoanalytic – which attempt to deny or minimize the extent of child abuse. A number of Miller's reviewers have noticed the absence of a distinction, in her work, between sexual and non-sexual forms of abuse, and I need not go over it here. What is especially relevant, I feel, is that where *Drama* took up the experience of some children, some mothers, *For Your Own Good* and *Thou Shalt Not Be Aware* are universalizing. Stemming from their need for 'power' and 'revenge', parents have a 'compulsion' to use their children as an outlet. The outlet is all too frequently sexual, only society denies it, and when it is, parents are acting from an unconscious compulsion to repeat their own experience as children. But notice that the experience that is re-enacted is real in the literal, narrowly empirical sense of the word.

Nevertheless, I have said that Miller's recent work includes a psychoanalytic orientation of a kind. It's shown in her deploying one form of the notion of the repetition compulsion, and in her respect for the arduousness of analytic psychotherapy and for the cathartic power of this form of one-to-one relationship to release the damage of the past. If my vocabulary is reminiscent of the language of early Freud, it is no accident, for Miller shares with Masson a commitment to the Freud of 'The Aetiology of Hysteria' – that is, to the period in which Freud attached to real seduction the power to traumatize. By the same token, she adheres to the 'cathartic' model of therapy – that it is repressed memories of real events which create symptoms, or create the compulsion to repeat, and that when these are worked through the patient will cease to be ill.

This is not to say that Miller's descriptions lack poignancy or force. The reductive theorizing of the two recent books – for her argument is essentially in the form of the cycle-of-deprivation, and she seems oblivious to the acknowledged difficulty with theories of that kind – is inseparable from an extraordinarily powerful indictment of a 'climate of cruelty' in child-rearing: from contradictory messages, deception and taboo topics, to outright physical violence and sexual abuse. Miller is also skilful on the 'denial of psychic reality' in children who can so little acknowledge their hatred of their parents that the hatred is split off and projected, and both parents and childhood are idealized. But to develop this argument she has had to make children into wholly good and innocent objects – as she puts it in her critique of the psychoanalytic theory of the drives, children are the mute receivers of adults' projections. Thus paradoxically, although Alice Miller is such an opponent of the idealization of childhood, she has ended up idealizing the child.

Miller's theoretical approach to child sexual abuse could be described as asymmetrically psychoanalytic. I put it this way because she does make use, as I've said, of certain parts of a 'Freudian model'. The past is determinant of the present. The parents have the greatest influence on the child. There is repression. Repression cannot be undone without the assistance of psychotherapy. But what are the implications of her view of the small child, for example, for a picture of mental structure or a theory of sexuality? Put simply, there is no sense of agency on the part of the child, in the most general sense. The notion of 'infantile sexuality', in Miller's work, is a defensive (adult) construct projected *into* the child to enable the adult to be relieved of (his) guilt about having sexual impulses towards (his) child. Yet it is a one-way process. With the child as recipient, there is no stage at which the child becomes a projec*ting* child; or at which there is a pre-existing mental structure which enables the process of repression to take place, thus providing the basis for the compulsion to repeat in later life. In short, the child has no unconscious mental life; only the adult does.

Actual seduction and analytic practice

Masson expected his work to lead to a deep crisis of confidence within the analytic profession, but it did not. This is only partly because his scholarship was seen as so easy to fault (Hanly, 1986b; Lothane, 1987) that his credibility was undermined. Analysts of more or less all schools have been concerned, since the inception of psychoanalysis, to establish general criteria for distinguishing between real and fantasied events (Merendino, 1985; Wetzler, 1985; *International Journal of Psycho-Analysis*, 1986), and specifically to go on exploring the conceptual relationship between the seduction theory and the theory of infantile sexuality. This is not to say that the balance was always evenly maintained. John Bowlby, for one, believed that the Kleinian emphasis on unconscious fantasy masked the impact on children of real-life experiences of separation and loss, and he regarded children's subjective experiences as largely a matter of accurate perception of an external reality rather than as derivative of unconscious processes (see Bowlby *et al.*, 1986).

But however divided the analytic schools have been about attributing causal or semantic significance to real or fantasied events in a general sense, none, to my knowledge, have been casual about the effects of real seduction. Take Anna Freud herself – ironically, in view of her later role in the Masson conflict – writing in the 1960s on child development:

> It is extremely unlikely that a child will outgrow his or her oedipal fantasies in situations where father or mother, either consciously or unconsciously, elevate the child to a substitute sexual partner or commit real acts of seduction with him. (Freud, 1968: 122)

Or, in stronger and more recent terms: 'Nothing could be more disturbing to a child than to have a parent attempt to realize these [oedipal] wishes by attempting a real seduction' (Hanly, 1986a: 216). Hanly, by no means a maverick within analysis, went on to despatch Masson, in the *International Journal of Psycho-Analysis*, in part for his distortion of the psychoanalytic view of the analyst's role. 'It would be painfully humiliating, confusing and profoundly detrimental to the progress of an analysis', he wrote, 'if an analyst were to treat even a distorted memory of a real event as though it were a phantasy' (Hanly, 1986b: 518). For one can believe in the existence of unconscious fantasy – and the notion of infantile sexuality and its effects is an instance of such fantasy – without being committed to the view that real seductions do not take place.

But psychoanalysis, as well as being a theory of the mind (or of mental structure, or the psyche), is a clinical practice, and the status of real seductions, for that practice, is pathogenic, for its impact on the individual at the time, and for its subsequent place in the work of treatment. Winnicott's view reflects both aspects of this dynamic:

> The greatest difficulties [in therapy] come when there has been a seduction in the patient's childhood, in which case there must be experienced in the course of the treatment a delusion that the therapist is repeating seduction. Naturally, recovery depends on the undoing of this childhood seduction, which brought the child prematurely to a real, instead of an imaginary, sexual life, and spoiled the child's perquisite: unlimited play. (Winnicott, 1961: 109–10)

Leaving aside for a moment the exquisitely Winnicottian emphasis on play as constitutive of a child's reality, these remarks strike me as representative of much of the analytic writing about real seduction. Childhood seduction is destructive because it is not appropriate to a child's sexual, physical and affective development, and it is the parents' task (or that of the child's carers if they are not the parents) to take responsibility for their own sexuality, and for getting their (adult) emotional needs met without using the child to do it.

But Winnicott's juxtaposition of 'real' and 'imaginary' takes the issue one step further, for it is a reminder that in psychoanalysis, the 'real' is always a paradox: it can be tangible or deeply intangible, observable or more purely internal. Most importantly, as Fraser's *In Search of a Past*, among other work, reveals, it is contingent upon the work of analysis itself (see also Safouan, 1983: 64).

Let me take one clinical example, which shows what was 'real' for one incest victim. It is taken from an article by an American analyst discussing issues of psychotherapy with hospitalized patients, including a young woman of twenty-four. The woman had had a sexual relationship with her father for ten years from the age of eleven, and was now hospitalized as a result of suicide attempts:

> I began to interpret to her that her self-mutilations and suicidal wishes could be understood as her attempt to punish herself for participation in the incestuous relationship with her father and to express her rage at him for crossing boundaries and taking advantage of her. She was perplexed at my line of thinking and explained to me that her father had made her feel very special and loved, in contrast to her mother, who she felt had rejected her. She went on to elaborate that she had become depressed and suicidal because her father had *stopped* his sexual relationship with her. (Gabbard, 1986: 341–2; italics in the original)

It is taken for granted that the incestuous experience is transgressive and pathogenic. In a situation where the young woman is attacking *herself* – her aggression is introjected – the analyst's focus is on working through an unconscious compulsion to repeat, here in the form of repeated self-mutilations, at a time when part of the patient's conscious experience is of depression and deprivation. Indeed Winnicott's point about the necessary reliving of a seduction, within analysis, finds an echo both in Gabbard's description of the seductiveness *of* the patient towards hospital colleagues, and in a lecture on incest in the Freud Memorial series at University College London a couple of years ago, given by an analyst of the British Psycho-Analytical Society who has worked with incest victims for a number of years.

'Why do you want to give the woman five-times-a-week analysis', I recall him describing one analytic colleague saying to another (both men) about a prospective patient, 'when her father's been fucking her every night for years?' That is, why couldn't the analyst 'leave her alone', why did he want to *repeat* the seduction, even if such a repetition were inevitable? There is thus a fine line, I think, between the arousal of narcissism or omnipotence on the part of the analyst (as is suggested by this example), and the space the analyst (or the analytic setting) offers for a sustained process of working through, not just of the pain from the past, but of what may have become a pattern of, for example, addictive relationships in the present – or no relationships at all.

Perhaps because it just rang true in a intuitive way, I have always remembered one other vignette from the same lecture: the incest patient who said to her analyst something like 'I had sex with my father for seven years, and it will be seven years before I can begin to get over it.' It is the notion of a process which cannot be forced and has its own tempo of resolution. It is only superficially akin to the cathartic as therapy, although it concerns damage at the level of the real event, for it eschews the notion of an immediate release of symptoms when a truth is realized (the patient is in no sense unaware of the real event in question).

One of the conclusions this leads me to is that analysts since Freud, far from blurring the distinction between real and fantasied event, have been *more* sure than Freud was himself of the destructive effects of sexual abuse. (Laplanche and Pontalis (1968) have provided what is probably the definitive account of Freud's uncertainties and attempted resolutions of his conceptual doubts on this score.) It is true that they work at a different level and with a different vocabulary from the language of a feminist analysis of power. They do routinely speak of 'actual seduction', not, routinely, of rape/violence. Equally they speak of seduction *into* the fantasies of the parents (Rycroft, 1984; see also Ashplant, 1987); seductive*ness* as a form of parental intrusion; and, in the words of a French analyst of, I would say, Lacanian persuasion and with an interest in etymology, of actual seduction as ending in psychic enslavement (Dorey, 1986: 326). They speak in a way that Masson never does, for in Masson there is what I can only call fetishism of the event – that is, of the physical or external event. As Laplanche and Pontalis (1968), among others, have pointed out, Freud's original theory distinguished between event and trauma.

When Masson and Miller replace 'seduction' with 'assault' or 'rape' or 'violence', an important distinction of meaning is introduced. Seduction always implies suggestibility (Lothane, 1987), or, in Masson's

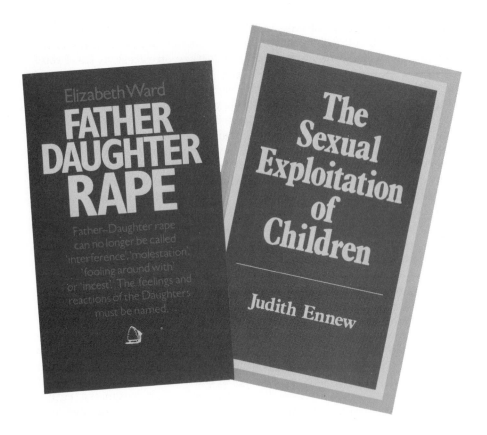

In contrast with the sensationalism of the Masson–Miller covers, the covers of Ennew's and Ward's books use typography only, but in different ways. The polemical purpose of Ward's book, and a sketch of its argument, are given in the cover text, with the greatest visual emphasis on the word 'rape'. The cover of Ennew's scholarly and politically committed book uses the kind of typeface seen most often in quality newspaper journalism and on the jackets of academic monographs. The title, although unambiguous, is laid out without titillation – or connotation or accent of any kind.

words, 'some form of willing participation on the part of the child' (1984b: 36). To counter what they see as the invidious effect of the word 'seduction', feminist writers like the Australian Elizabeth Ward (1984), who has documented the experiences of incest survivors, engage in this language shift deliberately:

> Freud moved from an initial awareness of Father–Daughter rape, to create an entire superstructure of metaphysical concepts in order to protect himself (the Fathers) from having to face the truth about the rape of girl-children by their Fathers. (Ward, 1984: 101)

We have returned to the problem of unconscious motivation, and thus of its description. Jane Gallop's formulation is apt, noting that 'as with all seductions, the question of complicity poses itself. The dichotomy active/passive is always equivocal in seduction, that is what distinguishes it from rape' (Gallop, 1982: 56). For it is always provocative to speak of complicity when sexual abuse is discussed.

I am reminded of the conflict between Erin Pizzey and the Women's Aid Federation, some years ago, about the legitimacy of speaking of battered women's complicity in 'addictive' relationships with husbands and lovers (see Coward, 1982). Because children and their parents are in an unequal power relationship (Ennew, 1986) it seems doubly provocative to invoke the notion in matters of child sexual abuse. In the words of Virginia (quoted in Ward, 1984: 57):

> Now I understand it as a power thing: I was obviously totally powerless to repulse this person that I was completely reliant on at the same time . . . I can see, as an adult looking back, that a child is quite unable to make choices about that contradiction.

In general I would say that the only way one could legitimately speak of complicity in such matters would be by describing it as unconscious, and as part of a most complex family dynamic. Take Gabbard's patient, who experienced her sexual relation with her father as in some way compensating for the absence of a relationship with her mother. It is almost a truism to say that the notion of a repetition compulsion makes sense only as an unconscious drive, for the repetition is so often of something psychically painful. Moreover, it is probably significant that the 'seductionists' in these debates about Freud do not seem to pay much attention to the later Freud, of *Beyond the Pleasure Principle*, in which the compulsion to repeat is posited as a cardinal attribute of mental life. In Miller the compulsion to repeat is a straightforward meting out to the next generation, a replication of one's past as a child. In analytic writing in the tradition of *Beyond the Pleasure Principle*, the compulsion to repeat is a more nuanced form of self-destruction or destruction of the other.

I said earlier that Masson's view involved a caricature. 'That is the worst thing that analysis has left the world,' he said in conversation with Janet Malcolm, 'the notion that there is no reality, that there are only individual experiences of it' (Malcolm, 1984: 55–6). It is a caricature because it inscribes a view which only the most solipsistic, relativist analyst could hold – and indeed it is a view which not many analysts show signs of holding. More common is the view that there is a reality out there, but the analyst's task is to enable the patient to understand how she or he is construing and misconstruing it, constructing it in such a way as to enact a role, such as that of victim, that the patient most wants to be free of but feels in thrall to. When I looked through the past few years' analytic journals to get a sense of the discussion of childhood seduction and its effects, I found little evidence to support Masson's view of a calculated indifference to the issue. It goes some way to explaining why analysts have on the whole appeared untroubled about the possible effect of his work on their practice, professional and intellectual.

Notes

I wish to thank Barbara Taylor and Bob Young, whose thoughts on the implications of issues raised in the first draft of this article helped me greatly in preparing the final version of it. An earlier version of the discussion of Alice Miller appeared in *City Limits* 21–8 May 1987.

Ann Scott is an editor at Free Association Books, London, and is writing a book of essays on women psychoanalysts, to be published by The Women's Press. She helped to organize the seminar series 'Psychoanalysis and History', held in 1985–6 by History Workshop, and is a member of the editorial advisory panel of *Free Associations*.

References

ASHPLANT, T. G. (1987) 'Fantasy, Narrative, Event: Psychoanalysis and History' *History Workshop* Spring, issue 23 (pp. 166–73).

BOWLBY, John, FIGLIO, Karl and YOUNG, Robert M. (1986) 'An Interview with John Bowlby on the Origins and Reception of his Work' *Free Associations* no. 6 (pp. 36–64).

CLARK, Ronald (1980) *Freud: The Man and the Cause* London: Jonathan Cape and Weidenfeld & Nicolson.

COWARD, Rosalind (1982) 'Erin Pizzey Adrift in a Misogynist Society' *Guardian*, 2 November.

DOREY, Roger (1986) 'The Relationship of Mastery', *International Review of Psycho-Analysis*, Vol. 13 (pp. 323–32).

ENGLISH, Deirdre (1984) 'The Masson–Malcolm Dispute' *Mother Jones*, December, Vol. 9, no. 10 (p. 6).

ENNEW, Judith (1986) *The Sexual Exploitation of Children* Cambridge/Oxford: Polity Press.

FRASER, Ronald (1984) *In Search of a Past: The Manor House, Amnersfield, 1933–1945*, London: Verso Books.

FREUD, Anna (1954) 'Problems of Infantile Neurosis: Contribution to the Discussion' in *Indications for Child Analysis and Other Papers 1945–1956* London: Hogarth Press and the Institute of Psycho-Analysis, 1969 (pp. 327–55).

FREUD, Anna (1968) 'Indications and Contraindications for Child Analysis' in *Problems of Psychoanalytic Training, Diagnosis, and the Technique of Therapy* London: Hogarth Press and the Institute of Psycho-Analysis, 1974 (pp. 110–23).

GABBARD, Glen, O. (1986) 'The Treatment of the "Special" Patient in a Psycho-analytic Hospital' *International Review of Psycho-Analysis* Vol. 13 (pp. 333–47).

GALLOP, Jane (1982) *Feminism and Psychoanalysis: The Daughter's Seduction* Basingstoke: Macmillan.

HAMPSHIRE, Stuart (1982) 'Comedy of a Freudian Showpiece' [review of Obholzer] *Sunday Times*, 19 December.

HANLY, Charles (1986a) 'Lear and His Daughters' *International Review of Psycho-Analysis* Vol. 13 (pp. 211–20).

HANLY, Charles (1986b) Review of Masson and Malcolm *International Journal of Psycho-Analysis* Vol. 67 (pp. 517–19).

INTERNATIONAL JOURNAL OF PSYCHO-ANALYSIS (1986) Panel on identification in the perversions, Vol. 67 [contributions by J. A. Arlow (p. 247), Harold Blum (p. 274), Kinston and Cohen (p. 347), Alan B. Zients (pp. 78–81)].

KENDRICK, Walter (1984) 'Not Just Another Oedipal Drama: The Unsinkable Sigmund Freud' [review of Masson, Malcolm and other new work on Freud] *Voice Literary Supplement* June (pp. 12–16).

KRULL, Marianne (1979) *Freud and His Father* London: Hutchinson, 1986.

LAPLANCHE, Jean and PONTALIS, J.-B. (1968) 'Fantasy and the Origins of Sexuality' *International Journal of Psycho-Analysis* Vol. 49 (pp. 1–18).

LOTHANE, Zvi (1987) 'Love, Seduction and Trauma' *Psychoanalytic Review* Vol. 74 (pp. 83–105).

MALCOLM, Janet (1980) *Psychoanalysis: The Impossible Profession* London: Pan Books, 1982.

MALCOLM, Janet (1983) 'Annals of Scholarship – Trouble in the Archives – 1' *New Yorker* 5 December (pp. 59–152). 'Trouble in the Archives – 2' *New Yorker* 12 December (pp. 60–119).

MALCOLM, Janet (1984) *In the Freud Archives* London: Flamingo, 1986.

MASSON, J. M. (1984a, 1985) *The Assault on Truth: Freud's Suppression of the Seduction Theory*, published with new Preface and Afterword by Penguin Books, 1985 (Harmondsworth: Penguin).

MASSON, J. M. (1984b) 'The Persecution and Expulsion of Jeffrey Masson as Performed by the Freudian Establishment and Reported by Janet Malcolm of the *New Yorker*', *Mother Jones* December, Vol. 9, no. 10 (pp. 34–47).

MERENDINO, R. P. (1985) 'On Epistemological Functions of Clinical Reports' *International Review of Psycho-Analysis* Vol. 12 (pp. 327–35).

MILLER, Alice (1979) *The Drama of the Gifted Child and the Search for the True Self* London: Faber & Faber, 1983.

MILLER, Alice (1980) *For Your Own Good: The Roots of Violence in Child-Rearing* London: Virago Press, 1987.

MILLER, Alice (1981) *Thou Shalt Not Be Aware: Society's Betrayal of the Child* London: Pluto Press, 1986.

MILLER, Alice (1987) *The Drama of Being a Child and the Search for the True Self* London: Virago Press, 1987.

MOSS, Norman (1984) 'Mastermind' [feature on BBC TV's drama series on Freud] *Radio Times*, 8–14 September (pp. 11–15).

NELSON, Sarah (1982) *Incest: Fact and Myth* Edinburgh: Stramullion.

OBHOLZER, Karin (1980) *The Wolf-Man Sixty Years Later: Conversations with Freud's Patient* London: Routledge & Kegan Paul.

PARSONS, Michael (1986) 'Suddenly Finding It Really Matters' *International Journal of Psycho-Analysis* Vol. 67 (pp. 476–85).

RUSTIN, Michael (1985) 'The Social Organization of Secrets: Towards a Sociology of Psychoanalysis' *International Review of Psycho-Analysis* Vol. 12 (pp. 143–59).

RYCROFT, Charles (1984) 'A Case of Hysteria' [review of Masson] *New York Review of Books* 12 April (pp. 3–6).

SAFOUAN, Moustapha (1983) *Jacques Lacan et la question de la formation des analystes* Paris: Editions du Seuil.

SCOTT, Ann (1987) Review of Alice Miller's *For Your Own Good* and the revised edition of *The Drama of Being a Child, City Limits*, 21–8 May.

STEINER, George (1984) 'The Fantasies of Freud' [review of Masson] *Sunday Times*, 27 May.

WARD, Elizabeth (1984) *Father-Daughter Rape* London: The Women's Press.

WETZLER, Scott (1985) 'The Historical Truth of Psychoanalytic Reconstructions' *International Review of Psycho-Analysis* Vol. 12 (pp. 187–97).

WINNICOTT, D. W. (1961) 'Varieties of Psychotherapy' in *Home is Where We Start From: Essays by a Psychoanalyst* Harmondsworth: Penguin Books, 1986 (pp. 101–11).

CLEVELAND AND THE PRESS:
Outrage and Anxiety in the Reporting of Child Sexual Abuse

Mica Nava

The phenomenon of child sexual abuse erupted on to the front pages of Britain's newspapers when it was discovered, in June 1987, that an unprecedented number of children in Cleveland, an area of high unemployment in the north-east of England, had been made subjects of place of safety orders and removed from their homes because it was suspected that they were victims of sexual abuse by adults. Over the following weeks the Cleveland story retained its status as important news and, indeed, continues to do so as I write and the official inquiry into the events there proceeds.

This article is not an attempt to establish 'the truth' of what happened in Cleveland, even if this were possible. What I want to do here is to explore the way the press tried to make sense of a phenomenon which had hitherto been kept a family secret, tabooed and disavowed, and which, as a consequence of media attention, grew over a period of weeks to occupy a position of prominence in public discourse and popular consciousness.

What conceptual apparatus – if any – did the press rely on in order to understand the issues on which it focused so much attention and anxiety? In what way – if any – did the shaping and selection of news contribute, not only to the way child sexual abuse was popularly understood, but also to the formulation and consolidation of a viewpoint which might be identified as belonging either to the left or to the right? To what extent were debates within feminism taken into account in this process?

In addition to addressing these questions, I want to look at the explosion of media preoccupation itself. Similar escalations of media concern have in the past been usefully illuminated by applying to them the notion of 'moral panic'.[1] These are likely to occur at particular moments of social crisis when people fear that traditional values and institutions are under attack. The media play a key part in sensationalizing the situation and, importantly – particularly in relation to the singling out of paediatrician Marietta Higgs in the Cleveland case – in identifying and legitimating the folk devils who become the targets for popular persecution. This process also includes the orchestration of 'expert' opinion which can contribute to increased demands for state intervention and the (re)formation of popular consent to a more conservative social order.

In certain important respects the Cleveland affair can be defined as a moral panic; and though it may not fit this definition in a predictable fashion, the way it does so is pertinent for feminists as well as for a study of the media. An investigation into how certain coded meanings were produced, and how Marietta Higgs was posed in opposition to Labour MP Stuart Bell, the other major figure in the controversy, can also offer an insight into the way the newspapers tried to establish for themselves a reasonably coherent position which would be consistent with their more general editorial policy. This was not an easy project, as we shall see. In fact, one of the most interesting things to emerge from an examination of the press coverage over this period is that despite the vilification of the tabloids – accusatory headlines and photos of Marietta Higgs dominated many front pages in late June and early July – a great deal of the reporting both in the popular press and in the qualities was characterized by confusion and contradiction.

This is not so surprising if one considers the deeply disturbing, opaque and unprecedented nature of the Cleveland events. Few other issues in recent years have provoked such acute dilemmas. The peculiarly complex combination of elements and circumstances in the Cleveland case has undermined previously reliable moral and conceptual schema, and it is not only the media that has been confused in its response. This has also been the case for feminists, for those involved professionally in the area and, not least, for the general public.

In order to formulate its stance in relation to Cleveland and make sense of the phenomenon of child sexual abuse, the press has had to evaluate the discourse and interventions of disparate medical, legal, social work, charity and psychoanalytical orthodoxies and practices. The 'experts' from these fields, upon whom the media rely in order to define and explain events, have themselves been deeply divided. Their conflicting interpretations have, in this emotionally charged instance, exacerbated the confusion of the press and made the task of 'orchestrating' and classifying expert opinion extremely difficult. In fact few other issues in recent times have done as much to reveal the way in which expert knowledge is politically inflected. To compound matters, the press has also had to take into account the views of politicians and of its readers. Politicians have not been a great deal of help. Tory and Labour MPs have not taken up consistent positions and new cross-party alliances have been formed (*The Times*, 29 June). Readers are not an easy constituency either: though they may be parents, they are also sons and daughters, and are as likely to identify with the survivors as with the abusers.

In many newspapers, the uncertainty that this lack of closure has produced has been manifest in the contradictory messages conveyed in different articles on the same page, and even within articles, as well as in editorials of different and sometimes consecutive days. The selection of objects of adulation and persecution – the targeting of goodies and baddies – has likewise not been straightforward. However, this attempt by newspapers to find and settle into interpretations with which they feel comfortable, this continual jostling of position, should not be read as evidence of infinite openness. It is important to recognize that the questions repeatedly posed, the solutions offered and the stories returned to, have all fallen within a narrow range. Moreover, they have been singularly neglectful of feminist argument.

Yet the paradox is that despite this, feminism has not been absent from the Cleveland affair. On the contrary, it has had an extraordinarily powerful symbolic presence in the person of Marietta Higgs. Whether this semi-conscious attribution by the press has been in the form of accolade or desecration, it has been there; and it has frequently taken the place of feminist critique. Certain clusters of meaning which have been evoked in references to her are evidence of this displacement. As the formation of a chain between Marietta Higgs and feminism begins to become apparent, we are reminded of the other more glaring association by which feminism, via Marietta Higgs, is linked to and even identified with the target of moral panic. In this way the spectre of feminism becomes folk devil.

How these chains of association and processes of displacement occur, and how, in conjunction with other associations connected with Stuart Bell, they might have affected the construction and appropriation by the newspapers of particular viewpoints on the Cleveland affair, I hope to uncover by looking in greater detail at some of the key moments and features of the narrative.

The narrative

By the final weeks of June 1987 the issue is firmly on the front page. The number of place of safety orders on children suspected of being victims of sexual abuse in the general area of Cleveland has risen to two hundred over the preceding few months, compared with thirty during the whole of the previous year. The orders appear to have been based only on physical diagnosis of sexual abuse (the reflex anal dilation test) made by two paediatricians at Middlesbrough General Hospital, Drs Marietta Higgs and Geoffrey Wyatt. It subsequently emerges, however, that many of the cases were referred by social workers and GPs. The abuse is assumed to have taken place in the home. The scale of the issue is brought to light when existing social service facilities are no longer able to cope with the number of children taken into care, and when parents of allegedly abused children demand second opinions and contact their local Labour MP, Stuart Bell.

By 24 June an 'independent panel of child-health specialists', which includes woman police surgeon Dr Raine Roberts, has been established to review the cases of suspected child abuse and concludes that there have been serious errors of diagnosis in seventeen cases; Roberts refers to 'the flimsiest of flimsy evidence'. This is the signal for a number of newspapers to begin to call in other 'experts' to evaluate the conflicting theories. What counts as evidence, social service policies and appeals procedures all begin to come under scrutiny, and there is a plethora of human interest stories, most of which focus on the anxieties of the parents whose children have been removed.

The disputed diagnoses also become the signal for Stuart Bell to begin to develop his public profile as the defender of misjudged parents. At the same time we witness an entrenchment of denials that incestuous child abuse has occurred. The response of the press in this instance must be contrasted with earlier reporting of phenomena like ChildLine, a help line for physically and sexually abused children, and the death of Kimberly Carlisle.[2] In these instances the press defended the interests of the children and called for more vigorous intervention by social workers. Now many of the popular newspapers, following the lead of Bell, who has claimed that *parents* have suffered many miscarriages of justice, turn around and call for the dismissal of Marietta Higgs and Geoffrey Wyatt on the grounds of their alleged incompetence.

However, it is soon clear that Wyatt is going to be a less significant personage in the evolving scenario than Higgs. It is her photograph that starts to act as a coded reference for the events of Cleveland, and her private and professional life that is examined in the daily press, not his. The Cleveland Social Services Department, with its policies of immediately removing the child from the family even where there is no evidence that the alleged abuse has been committed by the father,[3] also takes a back seat. It is Higgs who is attributed with the power and misguided dedication which then construct her as the causative agent in the crisis.

Over the following weeks Cleveland maintains an extremely high profile as newspapers respond to Bell's accusation in the House of Commons that Marietta Higgs and Sue Richardson, consultant social worker for Cleveland Social Services in charge of child abuse, have 'conspired and colluded' to exclude police surgeon Alistair Irvine from examining children suspected of having been abused. Media attention is bolstered yet again when Bell accuses Cleveland Social Services Department of exaggerating its child sexual abuse figures in order to increase its funding and 'empire build'. The story starts to diminish in importance, though does not disappear, once an official inquiry is conceded.

Denial and acknowledgement

Throughout this period many newspapers remain inconsistent in their reporting of the 'scandal' that they are themselves responsible for

The Daily Mirror *on the side of Stuart Bell*

promoting. What then are the contradictions which seem to have provoked such a crisis of irresolution?

Even for those not disposed to minimize the extent and the gravity of child sexual abuse, many of the Cleveland procedures have been deeply disturbing. Considerable anxiety has been expressed about the fact that, partly as a consequence of disputed – possibly exaggerated – estimates of the incidence of child sexual abuse, a number of children appear to have been arbitrarily subjected to a disagreeable type of clinical examination, the validity of which is contested. Social Services have responded to this disputed and apparently uncorroborated evidence of sexual abuse in quite inappropriate ways: children have been taken away, sometimes in the middle of the night, from their families, schools and communities. Parents appear to be refused access and have minimal rights of appeal. All this has caused suffering and it is not unreasonable to assume that the damage will be long term both for children and for parents.

Yet it is important to recognize that, although these worries have a rational and persuasive kernel, they constitute only a relatively modest part of a much broader position which is overwhelmingly characterized by denial and traditionalism. In this version, the seriousness, the extent, and sometimes even the existence of child sexual abuse are denied. The mythical 'traditional' family, and by implication the role of the father within this – the father as patriarch – is defended.

Thus, for example, in the *Daily Mirror* and in the *Sun* of 26 June it is defiantly reported that the children have suffered no other sexual abuse than that inflicted by the doctors who examined them. Michael Toner, in the *Sunday Express* of 28 June, asserts, without offering any evidence, that he simply does not 'believe in the avalanche of child abuse suggested by the Cleveland figures'. He also refers to 'fashionable' (i.e. not traditional) 'zeal'. A number of papers make comments of this order. Lesley Garner in her article in the *Daily Telegraph* of 1 July, entitled

Overboard on child abuse

The famil· unit can be vital to a child's welfare and should not be destroyed

From the Daily Telegraph

'Overboard on Child Abuse', prefaces an interview with Valerie Howarth, new director of ChildLine, by voicing 'the suspicion that we are encouraging, even inventing, a newly fashionable problem'. Awareness of child sexual abuse is being 'zealously encouraged', she says, and concludes by warning us that: 'Few people know what forces are unleashed once society begins to tamper with the mechanics of the family'. It must be noted, however, that Garner's succinct expression of denial and traditionalism is contradictorily placed at the beginning and end of a piece which, in the middle, gives serious attention to the views of Howarth.

Despite this kind of reporting, many newspapers do at the same time accept that children *are* sexually abused. This acknowledgement is what constitutes the core of the second, conflicting approach to the question. Thus although the press may express anxieties about aspects of the Cleveland Social Services response, it simultaneously gives a public platform to other professionals in the field whose arguments undermine the public denial of the seriousness of the problem. So from some newspapers it emerges that the rate of reported incidence of sexual abuse is growing all the time, particularly among children aged between three and five, and that abusers, who are overwhelmingly men and of whom a significant proportion are fathers and stepfathers, often intimidate children to such an extent that it becomes necessary to remove them to an environment where they will feel confident enough to reveal the details of their experience. In this view the family is not always a safe place, fathers (and sometimes mothers) can exploit the power they have over their children in astonishingly brutal ways. Survivors of incest and sexual abuse report harrowing stories of manipulation, threats of violence, long-term trauma and denial.

A number of newspapers express support for this general perspective. Among the most consistent is the now defunct *London Daily News*, which must be honoured for publishing early on one of the very few pieces clearly informed by feminism. Entitled 'The Sins of the Fathers', it argues that 'sexual abuse is the consequence of the way [boys] have learnt to "be men"' (Rutherford, 26.6.87). Other papers are both less sophisticated and less consistent. The *Sun*, for example, after running abusive headlines like 'SACK THE DOCS' (26.6.87), suddenly changes tack and acknowledges the existence of abuse in Cleveland in a front-page article entitled 'THANK GOD FOR DR HIGGS' (30.6.87) which is about a woman whose children were 'saved' by Marietta Higgs.

The sins
of the
fathers

IT WAS last summer, when
child abuse was again hitting
the headlines. I was walking
past a primary school, looking for the adult education
department. I opened a wrong
door and was met by the
suspicion and hostility of a
group of cleaning women. It's
not pleasant to accept that,
just by being a man, in the
eyes of others you are a
potential rapist or child
molester.

'WE BACK DOCTOR'

by PAUL CHESTON

Friday July 3 1987

Alarming increase i

The unknown victims

EXCLUSIVE   by CHRISTIAN WOLMAR and DANNY GILLMAN

CHILD sexual abuse in London has reached
record levels, according to a survey by The
London Daily News.
 In 11 out of the 17 boroughs which k
tics, there have been often dramatic
          cases

● Many cases still go unreported
● Youngsters used for sex videos
● Even year-old babies assaulted

The London Daily News *was one of the few newspapers with a consistent position*

'Dr Higgs was marvellous. I'm very grateful,' the woman is reported as saying. The accompanying photograph shows Higgs with a wry smile. Inside, however, the *Sun* reverts to its old self with an article entitled 'DOC IN "HUSH-UP PLOT"' which continues: 'Woman doctor plots with social worker' (30.6.87).

The *Daily Mirror* also moves backwards and forwards from an abrasively anti-Higgs position which denies the occurrence of abuse (this is the dominant approach, see e.g. 26.6.87 and 30.6.87) to one which acknowledges its existence (28.6.87) and, echoing Esther Rantzen and Michele Elliott who are interviewed in the same issue, argues in its editorial that: 'Helpless children must not suffer simply because we cannot bear to face the facts.' The *Star*, surprisingly, given its reputation as one of the most scurrilous of all the tabloids, carries a rather progressive and comprehensive analysis (see Alix Palmer, 9.7.87 and 31.7.87). Palmer's position is that current child sexual abuse figures are probably an underestimate and that 'Cleveland is not alone'; she is critical of government cuts in social services and the impact of these on

Contradictory reporting in the Sun

social-worker morale; she acknowledges the violence of many abusing fathers yet is also anti-imprisonment, since this is likely to drive the problem underground, and argues for a programme 'in which abusers can take responsibility for their actions'.

The *Daily Mail* coverage of the Cleveland events has also been extremely interesting. The paper is often accused of producing the worst

Daily Mail, Friday, June 26, 1987 PAGE 13

 Femail

BACKGROUND TO THE SCANDAL THE MAIL EXPOSED TO THE NATION

The making of Doctor Marietta Higgs, crusader

She trained in Adelaide, the city called the abuse capital of the world

WHEN a shy teenage girl arrived in Adelaide from outback Australia, the coastal city was going through a time of awakening.

Sexual abuse of children was no longer a topic to be hushed up — to be spoken of in whispers in doctors' surgeries and behind closed doors at medical conferences.

Hospitals were setting up special centres and appointing special : to cope with child abuse and the arch-conservatives County Wor Association was demanding heavier penalties for those who inter with children.

This was the prevailing medical climate when Marietta Higgs, three years out of school, began studying at the city's university.

She was already married and coping with bringing up two young children while still attending lectures towards her Bachelor of Science degree.

Her husband, David Higgs, was a medical researcher at Adelaide's Queen Elizabeth Hospital. Marietta upgraded her studies and went for a Bachelor of Medicine and Bachelor of Surgeries degree.

Devoted

She took her children to university each day, leaving them at the kindergarten in the care of overseer Pat Harlow.

She was devoted to her children,' Miss Harlow remembers. 'She was among the youngest mothers I knew.'

During her studies, Marietta befriended Antonia Turnbull, now a prominent Adelaide paediatrician. But as Antonia walked to the kindergarten Ones time to time with Marietta the girl who had come from the outback gave away very little about her background.

'I think I probably knew her

From RICHAI SHEAF In ADF

as a fellow studen anyone,' said Dr : many respects her at all. I was a family. But about the diff David had children whi their own cau

When M with what official Dr scribes as she ent childrens' compulse medical

Anr paed resp dec p

habitat
Sale

STARTS SATURDAY

10% off

Sofas a la Carte

AT LEAST

^% off

~om

Setback for couple in sex abuse row ... and a new controversy

PAGE 9

Freed children taken back from family

By ROGER SCOTT and ALAN QUALTROUGH

SOCIAL workers took back three children last night — minutes before they were to be united with their parents.

Immediately after failing to gain a further ... Teesside Juvenile care order to social services court, the applied to have the three made wards of court.

PARENTS: WE BELIEVE FULLY IN OUR DAUGHTER

Two of the children had days last ... looking forward and ... parents when they ... in Middlesbrough the ... Thirty of battered parents, knew nothing of the therapeutic ... ment, and the develop ... when they were told th ... Mr Graham Brown, the solicito representing the parents, said. The

only reason I can think of for this measure is that the medical services for treatment that the medical services they are seeking to continue cannot carry on because of the children

In court yesterday, the two girls aged five and seven and a six-year-old boy ...

two girls aged live and seven and a six-year-old boy ... Mrs Deverndt ... wife told the had allowed absence of the children had at home ... They did deny ... 55 had been in foster ... Wyatt, 35, days after ... brought Cleveland ... Earlier general social ... reveal another girl ... their custody at ... they were

Upsurge

Cleveland social services order on 200 children ...

Mr Wilkinson's ... that another 1 from ... may remove the new medical methe to their detained medical back to their ...

Her solicitor ... definitely said ... anything ...

In news ... was a ... only ... anything ...

Doctor under attack came from broken home herself

DR MARIETTA HIGGS comes from a broken home, it was revealed last night.

Her German mother and Yugoslav father separated in 1951 two ... after they went to live in Australia Marietta was ...

She was brought up with her younger sister Sonia by her mother who thought Dr Higgs's mother and stepfather.

And her grandmother, Marietta ... of those things of Dr Higgs's mother ...

'I can understand that both Marietta and the parents spoke to point she asks as Australian ... the family believed there was break would have, however, away from a child away from its parents ... stand up to do not ... at the same time can ... under-taking feel happened ... spend ... feelings car ... been married ... Canbott now there ... them ... could ... And they love ...

The Hattdays decided to

From RICHARD SHEARS In Perth

sell their story exclusively in the way Marietta was brought up ...

We have nothing to hide ... exposes her story to think the ... and has nothing to be ... their daughter ...

Smiled

Marietta Higgs as a schoolgirl in Australia

Fremantle 59, east of ... claims smiled softly as she ... children ...

You have only to look at the facts about children ...

Her hands have been ... for her daughter and ...

Fury of MP at choice of panel expert

Daily Mail Reporter

A WOMAN doctor who holds a controversial ...

love is...

... meaning

The making of Marietta Higgs in the Daily Mail

of tabloid writing (and is referred to in this way during the course of the Cleveland events by several of the 'quality' papers, see e.g. the *Daily Telegraph*, 1.7.87 and the *Observer*, 28.6.87). During the crisis it ran a daily cover line announcing itself as the paper which 'revealed the scandal to the nation', and had regularly sensationalist headlines. Yet at the same time it often devoted space to the views of Higgs's supporters, and oscillated in the position it took up. Perhaps more than any other newspaper, it presented us with contradictory messages – with both approaches simultaneously. Thus the portrait of Marietta Higgs (Shears, 26.6.87) is sympathetic – it describes her devotion, expertise and integrity – even though in the title she is referred to as a 'crusader' and Adelaide, the city she trained in, as 'the abuse capital of the world' (Shears, 26.6.87). Roger Scott (13.7.87), in a thoughtful piece, though with predictably inflammatory headlines, acknowledges the problems of Cleveland and weighs up the issues surrounding child sexual abuse as carefully as journalists in the liberal or 'quality' Press. At the same time, however, there are many pieces which use the crudest conventions of gutter journalism like, for example, the lead article on 30 June which is headlined 'THE CONSPIRACY'.

The *Guardian* and the *Independent* are among the 'quality' papers which, particularly in the early days, acknowledge increases in child sexual abuse. 'We must not recoil from the implications', argues the *Guardian* (25.6.87) while the *Independent*, though quite critical of Dr Higgs, states in its editorial: 'Talk of balancing parents' and children's rights is completely mistaken in this context. Children are not their parents' personal property' (25.6.87). (This position will not be adhered to consistently, however, as I will demonstrate later.) A number of papers carry letters critical of their own traditionalist stance; see, for example, the letter page in *Today* (27.6.87) which is headed 'Why Criticise the Child Watchers?' The *News on Sunday*, a left paper which claims to have uncovered the Cleveland affair in the first place and has always taken the side of the parents, carries similar critical letters.

What we begin to see then as we open the newspapers each day through late June and early July is the emergence of two quite sharply differentiated sets of assumptions and emphases, even though these are often not yet clearly identified either with a party political position or with a newspaper's general viewpoint. It is an indication of the absence of a coherent sexual politics both on the left and on the right that this confusion over Cleveland occurred and persisted. So given this lack of a politically informed guidance, how did the public and the press make sense of the events and make up their minds about where to offer their moral support?

Higgs and Bell

Very early on in the crisis over the Cleveland events, Stuart Bell becomes identified as the central representative of the first position

Accused parents' ordeal

● From Page One

and that the abusers are
dealt with."
  But he feared that in
the wake of the wave of
protests that had built up
over the Higgs-Wyatt
method it was possible
some real cases of abuse
could "slip through the
net"
  Dr Irvine said he was
speaking as an indi-
vidual but he knew that
the other seven police
surgeons in Cleveland
supported his view.
  He added that until
this year police surgeons
had been involved in all
cases of abuse in Cleve-
land but the previous
good relationship with
hospital consultants had
broken down since the
appointment in January
of a new consultant Dr
Higgs who had "strong
views with which I disa-
gree"
  In recent weeks, the
police had asked him to
examine a number of
children involved in sex-
ual abuse allegations.
  Arrangements had
been made but "at the
last minute I was in
doctors

abuse. A startling report warns that as many as one in ten children could be at risk from sex attacks.

But News on Sunday has uncovered almost 100 cases where parents, usually fathers, have been wrongly accused of molesting their children. The results are traumatic. In Britain

A FEAR OF LOVING
NEWS ON SUNDAY SPECIAL REPORT

May 3... How News on Sunday revealed the anguish of parents wrongly accused of child molesting

'They came for my kids at bedtime'

'At last someone believes them'

experienced   in   sonal attack on Dr Higgs   offices   and   support   totally   innocent   and
ex   done is to   groups is planned to   caught up in the system
          cope with the numbers   It was hard going to get
          so say they have been   people to listen to you.
            "I wonder whether the
            greatest abuse being per-
            petrated to children is
            not being done by those
            saying they are operat-
            ing in their interests
            when removing them
            from home on a just in
            case' basis
              "People have been
            coming to me

The News on Sunday, *left-wing paper on the side of the parents*

outlined above, that of denial or reluctant acknowledgement, while
Marietta Higgs is identified with the second. As the principal antagonists in this symbolic war of position, these two individuals will go on to
become critical forces in the formation of national ideas about child
sexual abuse.

Bell opens the battle with a salvo in defence of the beleaguered
parents, and in doing so singles out and targets Higgs as his main
opponent. It takes only a few days before Alistair Irvine, Cleveland
police surgeon, recruits himself as Bell's second-in-command and
further polarizes the situation. He contributes to the consolidation of
Higgs as representative of a particular viewpoint when he publicly
attacks her professional judgement and claims he has been prevented

SUNDAY EXPRESS

JUNE 28 1987   ★★★   PRICE 40p

EXCLUSIVE: Child-abuse row MP calls on Home Secretary for action

Marietta Higgs ... at centre of storm

Stuart Bell ... talks with Home Secretary

DOCTORS FACE

Higgs and Bell as representatives of opposing teams

THE
CONSPIRACY

‛ Dr Higgs and Mrs Richardson . . .
conspired to keep police out
of allegations of sexual abuse ’

MP STUART BELL YESTERDAY

**By GORDON GREIG, JOHN WOODCOCK
and ALAN QUALTROUGH**

A HOSPITAL consultant and a woman
social worker conspired to exclude
police from child sex
abuse investigations in
Cleveland, an MP
claimed yesterday.

Stuart Bell's allegations
against Dr Marietta Higgs
and Mrs Sue Richardson were
˙ ˙ked last night by the area's
˙nstable.

'˙˙˙˙˙ted to change
˙nd made
˙ Mr

The scandal the Mail revealed to the nation

Moore and Lord Lane the Lord Chief
Justice.

Lord Lane yesterday halted the cases of 20
children being dealt with at Middlesbrough.
The local hearing should have decided
whether the youngsters, all wards of court,
should be returned to their parents. But
Lord Lane ruled that the issue was so
important it should be handled by a High
Court judge in Leeds today.

In other developments yesterday: *In the
Commons,* Health Minister Tony Newton
called for an 'urgent report' into the affair,
in which the children have been taken into
care following examinations by Dr Higgs
and her colleague Geoffrey Wyatt. Many
parents say they are being falsely accused
of sexually abusing their children.

Helping

Mr Newton said ˙˙˙   ˙˙˙˙lines on
abuse ˙˙˙

**ACCUSED: Social worker
Sue Richardson**

**ACCUSED: Consultant
Dr Marietta Higgs**

The dramatic allegations against ˙˙
Higgs and Mrs Richardson were ˙˙˙
the ˙˙˙˙˙ ˙n emergency o˙

If ther ˙˙
˙˙ ˙   ˙˙˙   ˙˙

The women accused in the Daily Mail

by her from examining suspected cases of child sexual abuse. Irvine is
reported as saying, 'these doctors are seeing things that are not there . . .
Dr Higgs' methods seem almost to be an obsession' (*Sunday Telegraph*,
28.6.87). The other main recruits to Bell's army are the Rev. Michael
Wright, local priest and architect of parents' support groups, who writes
a poignant article for the *Guardian* (29.6.87) entitled 'When Fear Stalks
the Innocent', and local Tory MPs Richard Holt and Tim Devlin who join
Bell in making political capital by calling vociferously for the suspension
of Dr Higgs.

As the courts start to return children one by one to their parents
(though they remain wards of court) because there is insufficient
evidence of sexual abuse, and it becomes even more difficult to evaluate
the situation, a number of figures step forward to declare their support
for Marietta Higgs. The *Observer*, itself consistently sympathetic to her,
reports on a statement of support from a group of twenty-five women
doctors from Northumbria who provide a service to the police in cases of
child sexual abuse and who claim that Dr Higgs has 'lifted the lid on the
horrifying scale of sexual abuse from which we have averted our eyes for
too long' (*Observer*, 28.6.87). However it is Sue Richardson, Middlesbrough consultant social worker in charge of child sexual abuse, who is
appointed to the role of Marietta Higgs's chief second by Stuart Bell

himself when he accuses both under parliamentary privilege of 'colluding and conspiring' to deny access to the police in sexual abuse cases (all papers report this on 30.6.87, the *Guardian* reports Sue Richardson's denial on 1.7.87).

Stuart Bell escalates the crisis yet again, and adds new recruits to Marietta Higgs's team, when he points the finger once more, this time at Dr Jane Wynne, Leeds University paediatrician responsible for developing the use of the diagnostic methods employed by Higgs and Wyatt. Bell objects to her presence on the panel of child sexual abuse professionals established to assess Middlesbrough Hospital practice, because, he argues, her presence might threaten its impartiality. Another recruit to Marietta's side, this time more of a volunteer than a victim of Bell's conscription methods, is Esther Rantzen. Well known as a TV personality and for her involvement in ChildLine, her voice is heard in a number of articles and interviews (see *Sunday Mirror*, 28.6.87 and the *Sunday Times* 5.7.87), as are those of Valerie Howarth, director of ChildLine (*Daily Telegraph*, 1.7.87 and the *Star* 9.7.87) and Michele Elliott, author of *Kidscape*. Rantzen focuses on the distress of the survivors, Howarth on policy and Elliott on educational projects with children. All three express general support for Higgs. In the House of Commons it is Labour MP Clare Short who is most outspoken in her defence. Marietta Higgs and Clare Short are together accused in an astonishingly sloppy article by Ferdinand Mount (*Daily Telegraph*, 3.7.87) of being 'panic-stirrers' who have *caused* the moral panic by 'ventilating the extraordinary claim' that 10 per cent of children in Britain are sexually abused. Although Cleveland Social Services spokespeople also publicly support Higgs, as do a substantial number of medical, psychiatric and social work professionals, these individuals are not personalized in the press in the way that the women are. And they rarely have their photographs printed.

Gradually, then, two opposing positions begin to emerge in the coverage of Cleveland, though neither fits neatly into existing political frameworks or is easy to evaluate. What we see instead is the formation of opposing teams of individuals whose public image we feel able to assess quite easily. Over this critical period the public images of these two teams become inextricably identified with two opposing positions on child sexual abuse. Indeed, it is the team personality, rather than the issues, which appears to influence the press, and therefore the public, in their response to the Cleveland affair.

If this is the case, we must examine the crucial components of these public images. What do the different people represent? How do these images operate to produce and convey particular meanings? The most striking feature of the teams as I have set them out above is that one is composed almost entirely of men and the other almost entirely of women. It is rare that professional women are singled out for public attention to this extent and in this fashion. The very clear division made between men and women in the Cleveland case points to a possible

The doctor ...   ... and the social worker

Figures involved in the Cleveland controversy: Marietta Higgs and Sue Richardson, the doctor and the social worker, MP Stuart Bell who's sent a dossier to the Government, and police surgeon Alistair Irvine. But while the arguments go on a young mother cries on the steps outside a hospital ward ... her child is inside

The politician   The police surgeon

It would be inconceivable for a doctor as experienced as Dr Higgs to rely solely on the RAD technique without taking into consideration other symptoms in a child's health, to come to a conclusion so quickly that the child had been abused.

to establish a proper working relationship. The dossier shows that a meeting took place on Thursday, May 28 in Room 34 of the Social Services' headquarters in Marton Road, Middlesbrough.

War of position: the women and the men, from the Daily Mail

explanation of how the papers came to make sense, whether consciously or not, of what went on.

In addition to gender, each of the chief protagonists occupies other positions of symbolic significance. The meanings associated with these different positions need to be drawn out. Let us look first at Stuart Bell and his team. What does he stand for and support? What coded messages about him and his supporters are transmitted by the newspapers? How is his persona contrasted with that of Marietta Higgs? The first thing to note is that he is indigenous: a northerner, local, son of a Durham miner; salt of the earth, populist. The parents who he defends are 'his' people, he claims; his own five-year-old son, recently admitted to Middlesbrough Hospital after an accident, could have been one of the luckless children taken into care. He himself could have been one of the parents. For him and for his supporters, parents are an undifferentiated unit: fathers, almost always the perpetrators of abuse, are not distinguished from mothers; power relations are never made visible. Bell is a right-wing Labour MP: 'This is Middlesbrough not Russia', he is reported as saying in disbelief when he first heard of children being taken from their homes (*Daily Mail*, 15.7.87). Politically situated at the point where right-wing labourism merges into Thatcherite populism, he is against the growing influence of the left in local government and social services, and accuses his opponents of 'empire building'. I have already pointed out that his principal allies in the campaign to defend innocent parents (read fathers) are Tory MPs Richard Holt and Tim Devlin, the Rev. Michael Wright and police surgeon Dr Alistair Irvine. As Beatrix Campbell has said: 'These are the *traditional authorities*' (*New Statesman*, 31.7.87).

A number of quite different associations and prejudices are mobilized by the persona of Marietta Higgs. To start with, apart from being a woman, she is foreign and middle class – an outsider in Cleveland. We hear from the *Daily Mail* (27.6.87) that her German mother and Yugoslav father separated when she was two and that she was brought up by her mother and stepfather in a 'splendid' house in Australia. She is herself a working mother of five children and is unconventional in her domestic arrangements – her husband looks after the home and children. A number of commentators have hinted that these factors may have played a part in her diagnostic decisions (*Daily Mail*, 27.6.87 and *Daily Express*, 28.6.87). No allusions of this nature are ever made in order to explain the behaviour of Stuart Bell. Marietta Higgs is a modern career woman. She is personally neat, dignified, determined and professionally highly respected by colleagues for her dedication, integrity and clinical expertise. Many of the newspapers refer to this, yet it is almost as though these are coded references which simultaneously suggest that she is *too* conscientious and rather *too* clever – neither very English nor very feminine.

Worse than that, she is also identified with a group of younger 'committed' professional women and men in social services, with connotations here of the inner city, left radicalism and antipolice sentiment (see *Guardian* editorial, 1.7.87). Left intellectuals are also drawn into this network of associations when a couple of newspapers report that Sue Richardson is married to a lecturer in Humanities at Teeside Polytechnic. Oh horrors! Marietta Higgs's concern for the interests of children and her determination to uncover sexual abuse – described by *Today* (26.6.87) as her 'one-woman crusade' – construct her not only as anti-father, but possibly anti-men, possibly a feminist. This image produces another set of associations, and when these are in turn combined with her reputation as a conscientious worker, what emerges are numerous anxious references in newspapers across the political

The Independent *editorial*

spectrum to zeal: excessive zeal; fanaticism; obsession; fashionable zeal; fashionable prejudice, and so on. It is worth quoting the *Independent* editorial of 30 June at length in this respect:

> Social changes have made both sexual abuse, and the inclination to discover such abuse where it does not exist, more likely. Divorce, remarriage and the increasing acceptance of illegitimacy means that growing numbers of children live with a step-parent . . . forms of sexual activity which were, until recently, considered deviant have become commonplace. Lesbianism and homosexuality are now socially acceptable . . . Further, militant feminists are inclined to consider all men sexually aggressive and rapacious until proved innocent. The nuclear family, once the highest ideal, is now too often regarded as unnatural and unattractive . . . There is a danger that fashionable prejudice . . . [will] label parents guilty until proved innocent and break up families before rather than after abuse has been confirmed.

So here we have encapsulated the cluster of anxieties and associations triggered off by the persona and practice of Marietta Higgs. Modern fashionable ideas about sexual abuse are linked with unorthodox, dangerous ideas about sexual politics, with militant feminism, homosexuality and lesbianism, with the break up of the traditional family and with antifamily sentiment. Other newspapers make connexions with the left and with hostility to the police. The chain of meanings that is established here implies that ideas associated with Marietta Higgs should be treated with suspicion. In this conceptual manoeuvre the interests of the child, and her exploitation, are made invisible.

Conclusion?

I have tried to trace the way in which Marietta Higgs was transformed, through her media representations, into a symbol – a standard bearer – of feminism, and by association, of municipal socialism. It is important that we recognize this and understand the way in which newspapers have used her symbolic existence as a yardstick against which to work out their own positions. We must be aware of the way the Press has mapped out the field and controlled the parameters of the meanings that have been produced. If we are not, we run the risk of being pushed by the media construction of Marietta Higgs as the representative of feminism and anti-traditionalism into uncritically offering her our approval.

It is tempting to do this, because we have seen her become the target of a massive and violent seizure of misogyny. This public convulsion has been fuelled not so much by dislike as by fear: fear of the woman doctor, the professional woman, the woman with knowledge and public power. We have also witnessed an astonishing attempt by many of the newspapers, following Bell's lead, to displace the guilt for the sexual abuse of children from the perpetrators on to Marietta Higgs. Responsibility for causing the moral panic has similarly, by a remarkable sleight of hand, been removed from Stuart Bell and the press, and projected once again on to the unfortunate Marietta Higgs (Mount, 3.7.87).

Yet it is vital that we do not allow this powerful expression of misogyny to blind us to the problems in Higgs's diagnostic practice. Nor should Higgs's symbolic feminist presence be allowed to obscure the narrowness of the range of issues which were debated in the press. The marginalization of feminist critique is particularly disappointing given the body of feminist theoretical work on child sexual exploitation already in existence (and now augmented by this issue of *Feminist Review*). Few newspapers asked questions about power in the family or ideals of masculinity and femininity when they attempted to explain child sexual abuse. Similarly, although the press made token references to the 'rights' of children, there was very little discussion of what this might mean, nor of how the obedience and sexual ignorance of children might increase their vulnerability to sexual exploitation. With a few exceptions (for example, Weir in the *London Daily News*, 23.7.87) newspapers did not address the complex question of what Cleveland might represent in terms of the growing legitimation granted to the state to regulate and intervene in our domestic lives.[4]

Although it may be pleasing that feminism was so massively present in the reporting of the Cleveland affair in the symbolic form of Marietta Higgs, its vilification cannot give us much satisfaction. Although the issue of child sexual abuse emerged from its regime of silence and many papers engaged seriously with some of the progressive arguments, their continuous oscillation and the limited base of the debate do not amount to much of an achievement. As Roger Scott said in the *Daily Mail* (13.7.87): 'There is no black and white in this story. It is too complex . . . There are no winners. The children have lost the most.'

Notes

Mica Nava is a lecturer in the Department of Cultural Studies at North East London Polytechnic and a member of the *Feminist Review* editorial collective.

Many thanks to friends and family for their patience and support. Thanks also to Erica Carter, Peter Chalk, Catherine Hall, Angela McRobbie and the *Feminist Review* issue group for helpful comments.

1 See, for example, Cohen (1972), Hall *et al.* (1978) and Fitzpatrick and Milligan (1987).
2 Kimberly Carlisle was murdered by her stepfather and the inquiry into her death ended just before the Cleveland affair hit the headlines. This was one of the cases in which the Press criticized social workers for not being vigilant enough in their protection of children.
3 See the statement made by Cleveland Director of Social Services Michael Bishop and quoted in the Press on 26.6.87.
4 Although state intervention and the gathering of information about families is sometimes progressive and can benefit women, we cannot assume that this will always be the case.

References

CAMPBELL, Beatrix (1987) 'The Skeleton in the Family's Cupboard' *New Statesman*, 31.7.87.
COHEN, Stanley (1972) *Folk Devils and Moral Panics* London: MacGibbon & Kee.
FITZPATRICK, Michael and MILLIGAN, Don (1987) *The Truth about the Aids Panic*, London: Junius.
GARNER, Lesley (1987) 'Overboard on Child Abuse' *Daily Telegraph*, 1.7.87.
HALL, Stuart, CRITCHER, Chas, JEFFERSON, Tony, CLARKE, John and ROBERTS, Brian (1978) *Policing the Crisis: Mugging, the State, and Law and Order* London: Macmillan.
MOUNT, Ferdinand (1987) 'Children Need Justice Not Moral Panic' *Daily Telegraph*, 3.7.87.
PALMER, Alix (1987) '30,000 Children at Risk in Britain Today' *Star*, 31.7.87.
RANTZEN, Esther (1987) 'Listen to the Children's Cry' *Sunday Times*, 5.7.87.

RUTHERFORD, Jonathan (1987) 'The Sins of the Fathers' *London Daily News*, 26.6.87.

SCOTT, Roger (1987) 'How the Children Were Taken Away' *Daily Mail*, 13.7.87.

SHEARS, Richard (1987) 'The Making of Doctor Marietta Higgs, Crusader' *Daily Mail*, 26.6.87.

TONER, Michael (1987) 'Should a Father be Afraid to Kiss his Daughter Goodnight?' *Sunday Express*, 28.6.87.

WEIR, Stuart (1987) 'What if the State Kidnaps your Child?' *London Daily News*, 23.7.87.

Newspapers consulted

Guardian; Independent; The Times; Sunday Times; Observer; Daily Telegraph; Sunday Telegraph; Daily Express; Sunday Express; Daily Mail; Mail on Sunday; Daily Mirror; Sunday Mirror; Star; London Daily News; Evening Standard; Sun; News of the World; Today.

CHILD SEXUAL ABUSE AND THE LAW

Elizabeth Woodcraft

In this article[1] I want to ask some questions about the legal issues involved in dealing with children who are victims of sexual abuse. There are three main areas of concern:

1 What is the appropriate way for the authorities to deal with sexual abuse cases – should criminal proceedings always be considered, and why?

2 Once criminal proceedings have been embarked upon, what are the problems for the victims and what are the legitimate concerns for the rights of the accused man, the defendant? What are the wider implications for defendants generally? How could the proposed reforms affect the conduct of criminal trials?

3 Does either of the two possibilities – civil or criminal court – begin to deal with the underlying causes of the abuse of children by adults, and are we in danger of expecting them to?

I use the expression 'ask some questions' quite specifically as I do not feel able to do more than lay out some of the arguments and put forward a few suggestions. We are dealing with a very confused area of the law. Society must protect and be seen to be protecting young people from abuse, but policies are being hacked out in a haphazard way in response to individual crises. Worse than that, I fear there is a more sinister pattern emerging, which can be seen when the changes are looked at in the framework of all current proposals for change, such as those contained in the Criminal Justice Bill.

In England there are at present two ways in which the law can become involved in matters to do with child abuse: namely civil and criminal.

Justice her equal scale aloft displays;
And Rights both human and divine she weighs:
But laws no safety to the weak afford,
Unless the scale is balanc'd by the sword.

Criminal cases involve the arrest, the remand on bail or in custody and then the trial of the alleged assailant. At present, in the event of a not-guilty plea witnesses for the prosecution (including the victims) give live evidence and can be cross-examined. If a man pleads guilty or is found guilty he is sentenced within the range of permitted sentences, including conditional discharge, probation and imprisonment. Conditions can be put on an order for probation – that, for example, a man attend a clinic or therapy sessions.

Civil cases centre around the child. Wardship proceedings can be commenced in the High Court by a parent or a local authority, or care proceedings can be started in the Magistrates (Juvenile) Court by the local authority.

Civil courts

Care proceedings involve the local authority producing evidence, usually from social workers who have worked with the family as a whole or with the children only, doctors who have seen the children in their surgeries or in hospital and sometimes police officers who have been first on the scene. Police or social workers may even have initiated proceedings by taking a 'place of safety' order which effectively removes the child from her parents for one week because of the officer's or social worker's fear of danger to the child. Care proceedings can end either in a care order, with the local authority deciding where the child should live, or a supervision order, where the child lives at home and the local authority has a supervisory role.

The wardship jurisdiction is a much more flexible one. The court can make orders requiring a man to leave the home in order to protect the children, and women, of the family. There is greater scope for interested parties such as other members of the family to be involved in the case, and more enlightened decisions about where and with whom children are to live can be made. The custody of the child remains with the court; that is, any major decisions affecting the child, such as leaving the country, undergoing operations and education, must be referred to the court so that even if the local authority is granted care and control, its power is fettered.

When a child has revealed that she has been abused, the first authority figure to be informed is usually a social worker or police officer. Frequently, if the child is believed, the child is whisked away from home under a place of safety order. Social services will have to make a decision as to what to do next. Care proceedings are simpler and cheaper than wardship proceedings and it is my view that it is often for these reasons that proceedings begin in the Magistrates Court.

As I have said, care proceedings end with the making of either a care order or a supervision order (or, rarely, no order). There is no power in the Magistrates Court, in these proceedings, to order the man out of the house. The only power the court has is over the child. Thus, unless the local authority intends, for example, to place mother and child together somewhere safe, the chances are that the child will be removed from the home after the making of a care order. The result must be that the child feels that she is being punished for revealing what has happened. If at the same time criminal proceedings are instituted against the man, she may begin to feel that she has been the force for total destruction of her own world.

This prospect may be a powerful weapon in the hands of an abuser who can tell a child with some truth that if she reveals the secret she will be taken away, Mummy will be angry, Daddy will go to prison, and nothing will ever be the same.

It seems to me that a more appropriate use of the law here is to involve the wardship jurisdiction. Whilst, quite clearly, it is never possible to do away with all the problems described above, the High Court can more effectively deal with the difficulties. With the welfare of the child as its basic tenet, the court can order a man to leave the home; can require him to undergo therapy or treatment if, for example, he wishes to have access, and can direct the local authority as to what steps should be taken in dealing with the family.

There should be greater use made of the power to remove a man from the home. (It may be traumatic for him, but surely no more than for the child.) This would allow the child to feel that she has not been rejected by her mother. Moreover, it would in the same way let her know who is in fact to blame, and who is regarded as blameworthy by other people.

Family courts

Before turning to look at the criminal aspect, I should briefly mention Family Courts. There is a proposal – the popularity of which seems to ebb and flow for no apparent reason – that matters to do with children should be dealt with under one roof. At present, the prevailing view relates purely to family matters – care proceedings, wardship, divorce. The theory of the Family Court is not decided and there are many conflicting views as to how it would work.

The idea seems to be that proceedings would be more informed and have less structure. However, that informality can bring disadvantages for the weak and inarticulate. At present the difficulties are unresolved. As far as criminal matters are concerned, whether the child is victim or alleged offender, Family Courts are not thought by most people involved to be an appropriate forum.

Criminal courts

For those of us working as self-styled radical lawyers, issues of crime and punishment are on the whole quite clear. We defend the accused against the powers of the state because s/he will on the whole come from a background of economic, class, colour or sexual oppression, whose crime may be either to have been in the wrong place at the wrong time or, at worst, a direct result of the oppressed background from whence s/he comes. We argue against harsh sentences. In particular we argue against imprisonment because we see this as an ineffective method of dealing with offenders; it is harsh and inhumane, introduces young offenders to more seasoned hands and causes hardship to those left behind. Indeed when an offender leaves prison, the secure home life s/he had before may have disappeared.

Then we are confronted with crimes against women and children. As feminists, we have a particular perspective on the root cause of such offences – that is, the position of women in our society. These offences are the more extreme examples of women and girls being objectified and humiliated. We want the child protected, but we must consider the guilt and anguish felt by the child if a father is arrested by the police and eventually sent to prison (guilt and anguish which may be increased if, at the end of the trial, there is no conviction). What of the distress and guilt of a mother, who worries that she should have protected her child, but who has, perhaps, loved the man, and who has missed or overlooked the signs and, moreover, whose economic base is now snatched from her? How is the family going to deal with the absence of a father in these circumstances?

The answer might be suggested that this family minus the father needs support and counselling, as it would if the father were not in prison. However, once the man is removed from the picture there may not be the same urgency for local authorities, whose resources are already stretched, to provide the appropriate help. The man is gone, end of story – for the Social Services Department. The family will totter on, its dilemmas unresolved, until there is perhaps a breakdown with, possibly, receptions into care.

Are we prepared as feminists to say, in spite of all this, that we must use the sanction of criminal proceedings? Why should we say that?

Criminal proceedings are one public way in which society says 'this behaviour is unacceptable'. Heavy sentences, such as long periods of imprisonment, show the seriousness with which society regards the offence. (It would appear that Appeal Court judges are kept informed of what popular newspapers such as the *Sun* and the *Daily Mirror* are covering as topical subjects for discussion, be they attitudes to low sentences for causing death by reckless driving or low sentences for rapists. They use this crude guide as a way of ensuring that the sentence fits the crime in the eyes of the public.) Should we not support any action by the state which seems for once to take the issue seriously, which punishes the individual offender and makes an example of him in order to discourage others?

My own answer to that is: if the action is criminal proceedings – yes. Whilst these remain the recognized means by which society indicates that such behaviour is not acceptable, then their use should be sup-ported in general (subject, in individual cases, to the points raised above). If the action is imprisonment – perhaps. Imprisonment expresses society's antipathy to the offence. I would, however, advocate the use of other forms of sentence which go some way to assisting the particular man to understand his own behaviour and desist from it in future. A sentence of imprisonment can never carry such a sanction, although it may happen that treatment is undergone when an application for parole is pending. It may seem a floppy option – bit of probation, a bit of treatment – compared to the appalling life-long effects on the victim, but short of locking people up for life, there is always the possibility that they will come out and commit an offence again. (Of course, it cannot be overlooked that a man's colour can be the undeclared reason why he finds himself in the dock, and why proceedings are brought against him when another man might have been merely cautioned. For the purposes of this article, however, I am dealing with the specific issue of the logic of instigating criminal proceedings.)

Having accepted, even if it is only with misgivings, that we can support the use of criminal proceedings, we are now faced with a further dilemma; that is, the desire to see young victims able fearlessly to give their evidence and to be believed, and not subjected to unpleasant and abusive cross-examination, whilst also remaining concerned that a defendant (and all defendants in the future) should have a fair trial.

In the last few months we have seen, almost daily, horrific stories in the papers of men – fathers, stepfathers, grandfathers – who have abused young children in their care. It would seem from the reporting of these cases as if sexual abuse of children is on the increase. Most recently we have heard of the Old Bailey trial, at which the allegations made against the defendants were of organized sexual abuse of many young children over a long period. Then, more alarmingly, we hear that this case has been stopped, the defendants released without a stain on their character. Something, we feel, is rotten in the way that criminal trials are run if guilty men are allowed to go free because a nine-year-old girl breaks down in tears.

This much is true: it is often difficult, given our rules of evidence, to obtain convictions. This is because children are afraid to see the alleged perpetrator face to face in the courtroom. Many children are too young to be able to understand what it means to swear an oath. There is often no medical evidence or no third person to corroborate the unsworn evidence of a child. Given the length of time it takes matters to come to court, children can forget details of what has happened. Yes, says the government (of the Party of Law and Order). We shall have video links. And we shall have children giving unsworn evidence which is not corroborated. And we shall have videotaped interviews.

So, what is wrong with that?

Video links

The Criminal Justice Bill which is at present before Parliament contains a clause which will allow children to give their evidence, live, from another room, through a video link. The child would sit in a room with a relative or trusted person and a video-camera operator. Those in the courtroom could see the witness, live, on television screens. The lawyers and the judge would be able to put questions which could be heard by the child and which she would then answer.

There does not seem to be much wrong with this. The only disadvantage suggested is that a witness should have to confront the man against whom she has alleged this crime. That seems to be a small price to pay if the child now feels confident to give her evidence. However, a note of caution can be sounded, in that the section in the Criminal Justice Bill which deals with video links in the cases of abuse of children also contains a provision for such video links to be used to take evidence from witnesses outside the United Kingdom.

Where did that provision come from? What debate has there been about it? For example, who is to oversee the running of the case abroad, to ensure that there is no one else in the room prompting the witness? Who are these witnesses who cannot come back to the United Kingdom? If the problem is the cost of travel, we have to acknowledge that the cost of a video link is not going to be cheap either.

Unsworn evidence without corroboration

At present, when adults give evidence in court they either swear an oath ('I swear by Almighty God that the evidence I give to the court shall be the truth, the whole truth and nothing but the truth') or they affirm ('I, Mary Smith, do honestly and sincerely declare and affirm that the evidence I give to the court shall be the truth, the whole truth and nothing but the truth'). If a person is found to be lying, she or he is liable to be charged with perjury.

Children from the age of about ten or twelve who are to give evidence are questioned by the judge to see if they know the difference between right and wrong and if they can understand the solemnity of the oath. If it is felt that they do, they are allowed to take the oath (or, presumably, affirm) and give their evidence. In a case where a child gives sworn evidence and that is the only evidence, the judge will warn the jury to take care of convicting a defendant when there is only the uncorroborated evidence of a child. In theory if a child who has been sworn is found to have told lies she can be charged with perjury.

If the child is between the ages of five and ten the judge will probably feel that the child is too young to know what it is to be sworn, although the judge may find she knows the difference between right and wrong and knows the importance of telling the truth. If the child gives her evidence unsworn, there is a requirement that there be some other evidence to corroborate it. Unsworn evidence of another child cannot be treated as corroboration, although sworn evidence of another child can be. If the only evidence is that of a child, unsworn, then the prosecution fails.

The suggestion now (although not part of the Criminal Justice Bill) is that children who have not been sworn will be able to give evidence without being corroborated. This evidence will be capable of being sufficient for a conviction.

I have to say that I cannot subscribe to any major criticism of this suggestion. A child will not be allowed to give evidence unless she can tell the difference between right and wrong. The fact that she is not sworn seems unlikely to make much difference. A child of ten who is sworn is unlikely to tell the truth only for the reason that she is afraid of being prosecuted for perjury. Similarly a child who is not sworn will scarcely start to lie because she knows there is no penal sanction. Moreover, a recent Home Office study has shown that children of five and over are no more likely to lie than adults. Therefore so long as it is clear in what cases unsworn evidence is to be allowed, it seems an acceptable development.

Videotaped interviews

Another plan now being put forward, although not yet in any Bill, is based on American ideas. This is that as soon as possible after a child has revealed that she has been abused, she is interviewed and the interview videotaped. The interviewer is a trained person – possibly a social worker, police officer or psychiatrist. Questions are asked and, if necessary, models and dolls are used. In this way, the child describes, while events are fresh in her memory, what has happened to her.

This interview can then be used in two ways as part of the investigation of the incident. Firstly, the alleged abuser can be confronted with the interview and may then confess, thus obviating the need for a trial. Secondly, and this seems to be the plan as far as the Home Secretary is concerned, the videotape can be used as evidence in the trial. The nearest we have come to such a procedure in this country is the example of the interviews made by members of the Great Ormond Street Hospital team, videos of which have been used in wardship proceedings. These have been the subject of judicial criticism. Complaints have been made that leading questions have been asked, that the answer required has been made clear, and that ideas have been put into the child's mind. (I understand that changes have since been made to interviewing procedures.)

These are also the main criticisms of the video interviews which have been used in the United States for the purposes of criminal proceedings. There is still concern over the sort of questions and the non-verbal messages being given by the interviewer, and children have been found to try and please the interviewer. There is also a large question-mark as to the qualifications of the people who conduct the interviews. Will their expertise have been tested, and by whom? Only when an interview is on tape will it be possible to comment on these points. Seeing an interview on a screen is a very powerful way of receiving evidence in an age dominated by television.

Conclusion

Contained in the Criminal Justice Bill, too, is the end both of the right to silence which protects the weak, confused and mad in police stations, and of the right of the defence to challenge members of the jury, which is often the only way that black defendants can obtain a jury with black members. These changes are being slipped in with little discussion or debate. Thus, over and above the specific concerns outlined above, the worry remains that these proposals for dealing with sexual abuse are the thin end of the wedge. In the same way that the government used public concern about football hooligans to ease through the Public Order Act which has very serious implications for anyone who attends a demonstration, it is using concern over sexual abuse of children to slip through unpalatable changes. So, for example, if videotaped interviews, with all their inherent problems, are permitted, a very powerful form of evidence could be used in other cases. On flimsy pretexts such as illness or work abroad, witnesses may not be required to submit to cross-examination.

Thatcher's Government has changed the way people think about home ownership, shares and the National Health Service. She can change the way people think about human rights. We have no written constitution which sets down the rights of individuals. They can be given and taken away at will. In a situation where the efficacy of criminal proceedings can be challenged – on the basis of their damaging effect on individual victims and the wider lack of effect in changing the behaviour of society at large – we must ask what price we are paying when we push for the use of criminal sanctions. The price seems to be more nails in the coffin of civil liberties. This cannot be the best we can do to protect children from abuse. As feminists we must be prepared to look further for ways of dealing with an insidious social wrong which is daily committed against children in their homes.

Notes

Elizabeth Woodcraft is a barrister.

1 In this article I have taken as a premise that the overwhelming majority of child abusers are men. I therefore refer throughout to perpetrators of offences against children as 'he'. I also work on the understanding that the majority of abused children are girls.

POEM

Gina Betcher

Is it a shallow feeling
that you and I
together share
Water
ankle high
Foot
and ankle bare

Is it amongst ourselves
that you and I
together
can feel warm
United
as one
Alone together
we conform

Are we visible injuries
that you and I
together see
As we stand
on the shore
and share
the sea
Water
ankle high
Foot
and ankle bare

BRIXTON BLACK WOMEN'S CENTRE:
Organizing on Child Sexual Abuse

Marlene T. Bogle

The Black movement on racial oppression and exploitation in Britain was born out of the fact that no one but ourselves can fight for our liberation. But just as we have to fight against imperialism, and one of its tenets, racism, so as women we have to fight against sexism and male chauvinism which is part of our oppression as Black women.

Over the years, experience has shown us that if we are to play a part in determining our own destiny as women, and as subjugated people, we have to raise our own level of consciousness and lead our own campaigns. It was with this awareness that the first Black women's group was formed in Brixton in 1973, to organize around the specific issues affecting us. These issues were never discussed, much less taken up, by the already existing organizations in the area.

The lack of resources in the Black community made it necessary for us to meet in each others' homes for the first two years after the group was formed, as we had no other suitable place to do so. In 1975 we found a meeting place and were able to meet more regularly and to attract more women to the group. In the course of meeting and discussing some of the difficulties that were being faced by us and many other Black women in the community, a member of the group raised the issue of lone mothers and how, as a women's group, we could support these mothers who were often isolated in their homes with their children. As a result of this discussion a group was started in October 1976 aimed at bringing together unsupported mothers, both Black and white, and particularly the young and inexperienced, who were isolated in the home. Its function was to encourage these mothers to learn to work together in a stimulating and creative setting where their children would also be cared for. This stimulation enabled several of the women to return to college and some to part-time work.

Feminist Review No 28, January 1988

Whilst some of the women in the Black Women's Group worked with the craft group, others were active in other community groups and organizations in the area. We chose to work in this way as it was impossible to initiate any long-term projects, owing to the lack of a permanent base.

As Black women organizing we realized that we needed a permanent base inside the community, where we could continue to develop our ideas and provide facilities for women and children to meet on a regular basis. We worked for funding and in July 1979 we appointed two workers. The major task of one worker was to find suitable premises to be used as a centre; the other continued the work with the women in the community. It took a long time to find suitable premises, but the Black Women's Centre was officially opened in September 1980.

The aim of the centre is to provide and establish a permanent base where Black women in the community can seek support, help and encouragement in coping with specific problems which they may face in terms of isolation, poverty, racism, sexism and class oppression. Although the emphasis is on Black women, no woman who wished to seek advice would be excluded.

We have developed a bank of information which is made available to all those who use the centre. Other areas of development are a craft workshop, a crèche for mothers who use the facilities, and a library and resource centre specializing in women's literature and Black history. We also run an information and advice service on such matters as health care and legal and welfare rights for women. Through regular meetings, seminars, discussions, films and study groups, women who use the centre are developing our political awareness, enabling us to understand our particular position as Black women in this society, and to guide our practice in our struggle for change.

My work around child sexual abuse started in 1985. Two women who knew of the centre asked to use the space to start a Black survivors' group. They advertised the meetings, and fifteen women attended. They had had enough of the racism and stereotypical images that were portrayed again and again at predominantly white, middle-class incest survivors' groups.

Unfortunately, the group folded after some six months, leaving only three women to carry on this very important work. I concentrate on one-to-one counselling. This is mostly with women who now feel ready to talk about their abuse and abusers.

The majority of women who contact me have seen our telephone number on leaflets and other publications; some are directly referred through other women's centres or other voluntary organizations in London. There are also referrals from YTS schemes and social services in Lambeth, which seem to be lacking in social workers with the necessary experience in sexual abuse cases.

We feel that statutory bodies use us at their convenience and when it suits them. They refer to us cases which they cannot manage, and they come to us for advice on specific cases, but they do not open themselves to the criticism, advice and help we could offer them to develop a more appropriate service to Black children and adult incest survivors. We see ourselves as women who have the experience and expertise to make a valuable contribution to policy and practice within statutory organizations, as well as working alongside them. This would not usurp their power. This state of affairs leaves us feeling exploited and taken for granted.

Our help is desperately needed and we cannot give up on the women and young people coming to us for help, but the centre receives no extra funding for this important work. The work therefore has to be done outside of and sometimes during my normal working hours (as in the case of telephone counselling.) There is also the additional strain of being responsible for and bearing the whole burden of counselling and advising often vulnerable women without the backup of an organization which is ultimately responsible.

The majority of women who contact the centre were abused during childhood, so there is no need to inform social services or obtain police involvement. More recently children and young people have been referred to us for counselling but social workers deal with the statutory side. This has alleviated a lot of anxiety because our past history of relations with the police has left its mark on the Black community. Black women, in trying to protect their own children, face racism from the police which can compound the abuse already suffered by the children. Black mothers do not want to put their children through this, yet they wish to get justice for their children. They find themselves in a cleft stick wondering whether to go for police involvement or not. Social Services are often not sympathetic to the quandary that mothers and children feel on this question.

The Black Women's Centre has had to organize around child sexual abuse because although sexual abuse has been an issue in the context of the women's liberation movement, it has for a long time been portrayed and dealt with as a 'white' problem. Books that have been written on the subject have ignored and excluded any experiences of what it means to be a Black survivor. All the myths, stereotypes and racism that surround child sexual abuse have portrayed incest as problematic only for white women and children. Black women did not have a place in this because of the racism inherent in explanations of child sexual abuse. Incest has been seen and believed to be the norm within the Black culture and way of life. This is not true.

Black women and children do *not* expect to be sexually abused as a normal part of life. To dismiss this myth one has to be factual and say that child sexual abuse does not know race, class and creed. It is an international issue and affects us all. What has to be understood is that what it means to have been abused is different for each incest survivor, dependent on their other experiences. Black women survivors have the experience of racism as a factor in the meaning for them. It was recognition of this which started the work on sexual violence of the Black Women's Centre.

Notes

Marlene Bogle is centre co-ordinator at Brixton Black Women's Centre.

This article is a modified version of a paper given at a conference in April 1987: 'Child Sexual Abuse: Towards a Feminist Professional Practice'.

BRIDGING THE GAP: Feminist Development Work in Glasgow

Patricia Bell and Jan Macleod

In 1981 Strathclyde Rape Crisis Centre was overstretched and under-resourced, not an unusual position for voluntary and feminist organizations. In amongst the individual counselling, administration, volunteer training, talks and fund-raising, we spent hours agonizing over two main points. Firstly, what did we have to offer the many women who, with great courage, were coming to us to talk about their experiences of sexual abuse as children? What on earth could we do to meet this 'new' demand? Secondly, why were we left to pick up the pieces after women had been to the police, courts, GP, or social worker? Why did women have to suffer 'secondary' abuse through the unsympathetic attitudes they often had to face? How could we influence the few specialist services provided within statutory organizations and so try to avoid women being further abused by the system? Why, when we had so few resources, were we supporting field workers who were in contact with abused women and children, whilst their own departments had nothing to offer them? The women's support project grew from these concerns.

In the Centre, crisis work had always gained priority at the expense of educational and development work. We felt as if we had the ideas and the experience to back them up, if only we had the time and resources to implement them. We decided to attempt to bridge the gap between ourselves and similar feminist organizations and the 'professionals'; we began to plan the Women's Support Project. From its beginning in October 1983 the project, which is urban-aid funded, has grown to employ three workers. It is based in the east end of Glasgow.

The style and direction of the project had to change considerably over its first two years. A main initial aim was to 'encourage women to make greater use of locally available services'. We soon found there were

no services available. We had thought that we could offer some individual counselling and advice work but it became clear that this would swamp the project and repeat the situation of the Rape Crisis Centre. Our job became to stimulate the development of services and to work at keeping women on the agenda of services which, at worst, have women-blaming responses and, at best, are prepared to refer people on.

The main threads of our approach have always been a feminist analysis of male violence, maintaining strong links between the causes and effects of rape, domestic violence, incest and child sexual abuse. We have been quite prepared to use any openings and jump on most (but not all) bandwagons in order to 'bridge the gap' and put our views across.

People can easily persuade themselves that domestic violence is a private, family matter and that battered women choose to stay in a violent relationship. We often have to point out that domestic violence abuses children too before people will take the issue seriously. We build on discussions of domestic violence before talking about incest and child sexual abuse. This is partly to minimize the mother-blaming which goes on whenever child sexual abuse is raised, but also to give workers a social and political framework with which to make sense of the day-to-day problems they face. In addition, people feel more comfortable discussing domestic violence since it is a more familiar area than child sexual abuse. This enables us to draw crucial links between the two areas, implicitly challenging male power, particularly within the family.

Our experience of training has convinced us that what is needed is not just clearer guidelines or more procedures but changes in attitudes.

To put it bluntly, there is no point in giving people procedures if they don't believe incest happens or think it is not their job to deal with it.

Workers find it difficult to admit that, as 'professionals', they feel deskilled and unable to cope. In trying to isolate themselves from the painful issues, they often separate themselves from the clients who have this problem. Child sexual abuse is not an easy area to work in. The issues involved challenge our personal beliefs and attitudes. Even with the most concerned and sympathetic of adults there is a great pressure to shy away from the possibility of abuse. A great many adults have been sexually abused themselves as children and, whilst personal experience can make you alert to the signs of abuse, carrying painful memories can be an added pressure against raising the issue. Our training aims to break down these professional barriers to make people face their feelings.

We often begin by getting workers to do an exercise on 'burnout'. They are asked to look at their own work situations and answer the following questions: what do you feel, what do you say, what do you do, and, finally, why do you stay? This brings out points such as feelings of inadequacy, exhaustion and failure and, at the same time, a sense of commitment to some areas of the job, the need for money and workers' fears of making changes. The last heading is then changed to 'why does she stay?' and the point is made that the feelings identified by the workers themselves are very similar to those expressed by battered women. The exercise is extremely effective in making people realize that it is not easy to leave a situation even when you know it is not doing you any good, and so makes workers less quick to condemn women for staying in a violent relationship.

We also roleplay a disclosure of child sexual abuse to make workers look at the way they are treating people, how they would want to be treated, and how the service they provide could be more appropriate and responsive to the needs of women and children. In the words of the Incest Survivors' Campaign, we are asking people to look at what they offer, and ask at every stage, 'who benefits, and who has to pay?' There is no doubt that that approach to training is very effective. People are less likely to blame incest on the mother, alcohol, children, unemployment or overcrowding and more likely to face up to the position of women and children in our society. Once this has happened, workers can then look at alternative responses to the problem, such as supporting mothers, working with the child within the home, and removing the abuser.

Violence against women and children, whether in or out of the home, is not a minority problem. The social position of women and children encourages their daily exploitation. Child sexual abuse exists on such a scale that we need a totally new approach to the problem. Voluntary services cannot meet the need and neither can limited specialist projects run by a handful of experts. In order to respond adequately, we need a community-based response which recognizes the relative powerlessness of women and children and does something to address this. This may involve people in reviewing their whole approach to their work, and facing difficult choices. For example, staff in a community-based project backed away from a campaign on domestic

Mothers

violence in case it upset their relationships with local community activists who were overwhelmingly men. What does this say about the value placed on women in the community?

Channelling resources into specialist centres and individual treatment whilst changing nothing else allows everyone to collude with abuse. It avoids challenging the power of men in families, the power of professionals over clients, the power of adults over children. It particularly ignores the fact that many existing services for children condone, ignore or in some cases actively encourage an environment which is in direct contradiction to any claim of prioritizing children's needs or encouraging their development. For example, workers involved with teenagers in care wanted to start self-help groups for girls who had disclosed previous sexual abuse. They encouraged the girls to talk but had no way of explaining to those same girls why they had to put up with male staff touching them, making sexual comments and commenting on their dress and appearance. Again, teachers involved in the 'preventive' work of encouraging children to be assertive and to stand up to potential abusers decided not to let the children use roleplay because it would 'undermine discipline'.

It is clear that child sexual abuse is an area in which theory greatly influences practice and this is why much of our work concentrates on making people look at their attitudes. It is also important to offer practical suggestions for ways in which workers can build up confidence and skills and develop support networks both for themselves as workers and for those who are suffering abuse. It is common for people to feel so overwhelmed by the scale of the problems that they don't know where to start. We have found it important to point out that very small steps can make an impact. For example, having leaflets and posters on display helps women to realize that sexual abuse is a subject that they can discuss. Having relevant books or games available helps workers to raise the general issues with children in a non-threatening way. We are presently working on a puppet show for showing to children under five. And, of course, workers feel more confident in approaching women and children if they are aware that back-up support and information is available for themselves, and so are reassured to hear of the work of voluntary organizations such as Women's Aid, Rape Crisis and Action Against Incest.

Towards this we have built up a wide range of books, videos and resource material. We have developed links with local community groups, offering information on violence, health and regular self-defence and discussion classes. We are continuing to run training courses, mainly with social workers, health centres and nursery staff. This often involves producing new material, since there is little available. We hope to develop a 'complete' training package which could then be used by training officers within these organizations.

Another way in which we try to break down professional barriers is in encouraging different agencies to communicate and work together more, and in developing inter-agency contacts. No one agency can deal with all aspects of a child abuse case. If each agency has a different theory, approach and level of 'proof', how does this appear to the child? Can you think of any way to justify this situation to a child?

For example, in conjunction with Glasgow Women's Aid we have organized 'Local Information Initiatives' on the problem of male violence. These have brought together interested workers from a variety of backgrounds and have provided a useful forum both for examining local social work practice and for highlighting gaps in information and service provision. A multi-disciplinary working party made up of local field workers has been meeting regularly to share and develop ideas and experience. This group brings together nursery nurses, teachers, health visitors, social workers, community workers and workers from voluntary organizations to discuss issues around violence against women and children and look at local service provision. Recently this group has produced five detailed information leaflets on 'Working with Abused Children'.

The work we do is often exhausting in every sense, but it can also be very exciting. Individual crisis work is largely invisible, but with development work the results are more tangible and easier to build on.

More and more resources are now being released to tackle the problems of child sexual abuse. It is important that feminists have the opportunity to do more development work, using the experience gained through individual counselling work, so that developing services are appropriate and begin to tackle the real needs as identified by the women and children themselves.

The project provides an opportunity for experience gained through involvement in feminist collectives to be used in helping fieldworkers gain confidence in dealing with the problem of male violence. In doing this the project does walk a tightrope and has frequently been in the uncomfortable position of being criticized and condemned by both the establishment and the feminist community simultaneously. Opportunities to discuss this problem and share experiences are limited, as we do not know of other projects doing similar work. We hope to see more of such projects; the only effective way to tackle the many manifestations of male violence is to stimulate a community response equal to the scale of the problem.

Notes

Patricia and Jan are feminists who have been working against violence against women in Scotland for the last ten years. Both were members of the Strathclyde Rape Crisis Collective before becoming full-time workers with the project.

Women's Support Project, Newlands Centre, 871 Springfield Road, Glasgow G40 3EL. Tel: 041–554 5669.

Drawings by Kerry.

CLAIMING OUR STATUS AS EXPERTS: Community Organizing

Norwich Consultants on Sexual Violence

In November 1985 the Norwich refuge (Leeway) organized an action and issued a press statement following the murder of Balwant Kaur in the Brent Asian Women's refuge. After some discussions with our local council, a working group attached to our Equal Opportunities Committee was set up to look at violence against women and girls. Representatives from Leeway refuge, Norwich Rape Crisis, Norwich Women's Centre and the local hostel for young women now meet here with representatives from statutory and voluntary agencies. This group has provided both a public forum for discussion of sexual violence and a route for achieving some of the changes many of us have been discussing for years.

Both Leeway and Rape Crisis had been discussing issues of policy with the police for many years, but with little positive outcome. The early meetings of the working group focused on the role of the police and courts in relation to sexual violence, using the recommendations of the Cabinet Office Women's Commission report (1986) as a baseline. The changes in police practice which have subsequently occurred are the outcome both of the 'status' of the working group and of the current climate of change within the police in relation to sexual violence: within six months we were told that a small room had been decorated and furnished, and that all women reporting sexual assault to the police would be interviewed there – the provincial version of a 'rape suite'. Interviews are now conducted by specially trained women officers. Recently, specialist workers in social services reached an agreement with the police that child sexual abuse 'disclosure' interviews should be done in partnership. Most now take place outside the police station in specially equipped children's rooms with video facilities.

We raised the issue of women police surgeons early in our discussions. The police seemed to have no objections in principle, but argued that there were no women doctors who wished to be full-time

Feminist Review No 28, January 1988

police surgeons. The possibility of having a pool of women doctors who deal only with sexual assault cases was raised, whilst at the same time a formal letter from the working group was sent out through the Family Practitioners Committee asking if any women doctors might be interested in this work. The initial resistance of the police to the pool system shifted when we were able to state that twelve women doctors had already expressed interest. An exploratory meeting was arranged at Norwich City Hall at which the police explained to the women doctors what would be involved. Two months later eight of these women had been trained in forensic practice at Hendon and were 'on call' for all sexual assault cases in Norfolk. We have heard informally that the system is working well.

There have also been changes achieved in relation to domestic violence: injunctions are now recorded on the police computer and officers are required to fill in report forms on all 'domestic disputes', which are monitored by supervisors. We were recently given the first statistics from these forms which showed that in about 10 per cent of cases this year the man was arrested – our police representative noted, somewhat ironically, that this was probably 100 per cent more than previously!

We have also had discussions with court officials about the organization of the courts, and ways in which appearing in court might be made a less traumatic experience for women and girls. Unfortunately a new county court has just been opened in Norwich, which repeats all the planning problems that feminists have been pointing out for years: huge open-plan waiting areas, the siting of the witness box opposite where the accused sits, and no facilities for children. We were told we should have raised these issues during the planning stages and that an official report from the National Association of Victim Support Schemes has recommended that in all future court buildings separate waiting areas should be provided for defence and prosecution witnesses respectively. Feminists should find out if there are plans for new court buildings in their area and make representations at the planning stages.

One intractable problem we have encountered is the training of judges and magistrates in relation to sexual violence. Despite recommendations in the Women's Commission report and many other calls for such training, the 'independence of the judiciary' is always cited at the local level as the reason why such training cannot take place. It looks as though only a directive from the Home Office will open up possibilities here.

The working group has also looked in depth at local housing policy and local media reporting. Whilst Norwich City Council has always implemented the Housing (Homeless Persons) Act in relation to battered women, a commitment was also given to the working group in relation to women council tenants who have been sexually assaulted. In practice this means that any woman council tenant who is raped in or near her own home, or any mother whose children are abused in the household, will be granted a transfer if she wants one.

Before our meeting with representatives of the local press we monitored the local papers for six months and one woman from Norwich Rape Crisis compiled a detailed report. Whilst the press representatives themselves were extremely defensive at the meeting (the local NUJ branch had passed a motion rejecting the report the night before the meeting!) the report was considered so thorough that it was referred on to the City Council Policy Committee.

The working group has also sponsored the production of an information leaflet, 'No-One Deserves To Be Abused', which covers rape and sexual assault, incest and sexual abuse, domestic violence and sexual harassment, which has been widely distributed in the city. A card was also printed which has the refuge number on one side and Rape Crisis on the other. All police constables in Norfolk now carry these cards, and an official memo was issued which suggests that these should be given to any woman or girl who might need this information. The Equal Opportunities Committee funds a weekly open advice session on 'Violence to Women and Girls' which is staffed by women from the refuge and Rape Crisis.

The most recent project to emerge out of the working group was an open training day for professionals and others on 'Violence to Women and Girls'. The day was planned, organized and facilitated by fifteen women from a range of Norwich women's groups. We felt it was important to make feminist expertise visible in the current climate of concern, and to ensure that it informed and influenced discussions of any changes in professional policy and practice. After much discussion and debate we decided to call ourselves 'Norwich Consultants on Sexual Violence'. We spent many hours working together on what we should cover on the training day and encouraging each other to feel confident about our knowledge and expertise. We eventually developed a very structured programme for the day. Leaflets and application forms were sent to doctors, nurses and other health workers, social workers, the police, probation officers, lawyers, teachers, trade unions, advice agencies and other voluntary organizations. Almost a hundred people registered for the training day, which took place in City Hall.

The day opened with lectures by two feminist researchers which set out a framework for the workshops which followed. For the first two workshops we mixed representatives from different professions and agencies. The objective was to create inter-agency awareness of respective practice and contacts for future networking. We asked participants to work in small groups in order to arrive at definitions of various forms of sexual violence and to estimate incidence. We finished the discussion by distributing a prepared sheet with our definitions and with incidence figures from recent research. We then moved on to discussing attitudes, perceptions and stereotypes of who experiences sexual violence, who commits it and why it happens. Whilst we had been pleasantly surprised by how close the participants' definitions were to ours, this second exercise revealed the tenacity and prevalence of stereotypes and 'commonsense' opinions when it comes to explaining sexual violence.

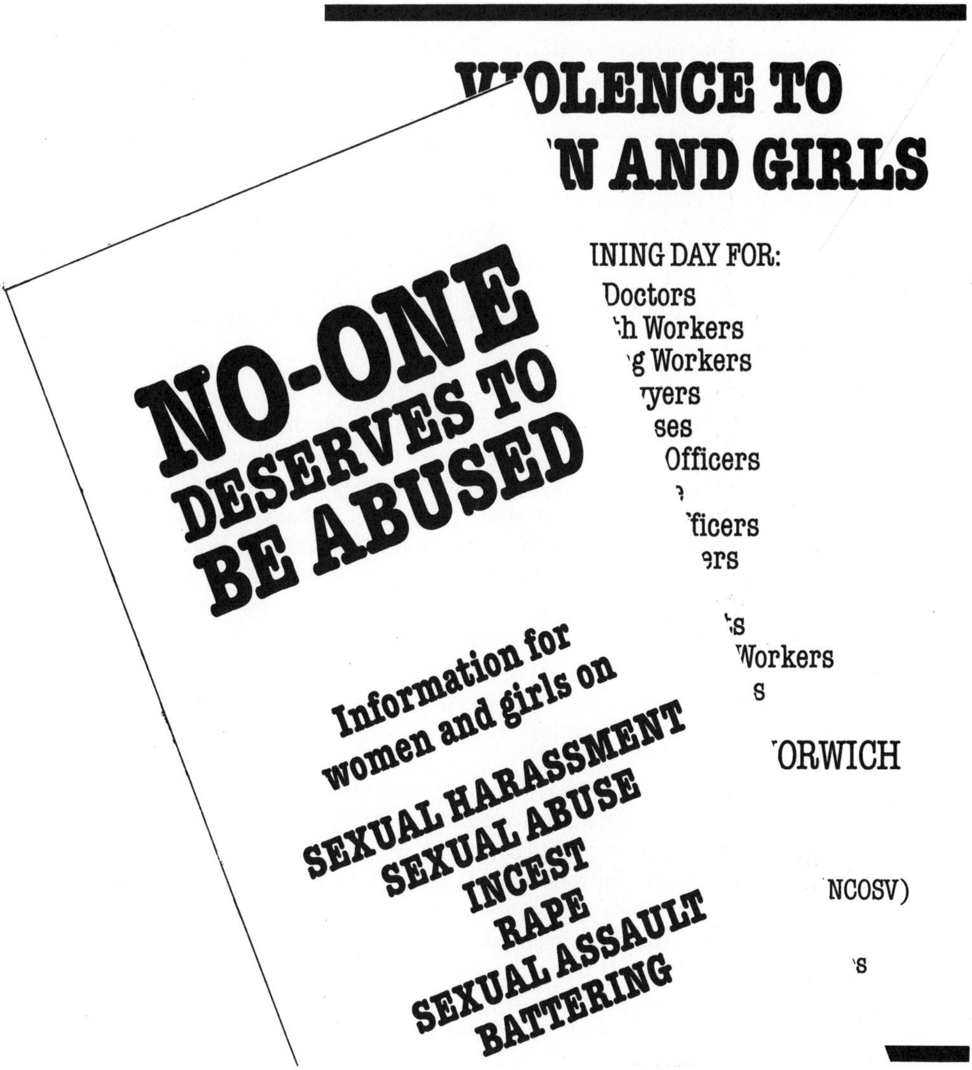

V'OLENCE TO
'N AND GIRLS

INING DAY FOR:

Doctors
'h Workers
'g Workers
ryers
ses
Officers
?
'ficers
ers

's
Workers
s

'ORWICH

NCOSV)

's

NO-ONE
DESERVES TO
BE ABUSED

Information for
women and girls on

SEXUAL HARASSMENT
SEXUAL ABUSE
INCEST
RAPE
SEXUAL ASSAULT
BATTERING

The second workshop used short case-history examples of a number of forms of sexual violence in order to elicit what is current professional practice and then to work towards defining some general principles of 'good practice'. The intention was to encourage participants to use their theoretical understanding of definitions and prevalence figures in their practical work within their respective professional contexts. For the third workshop participants from the same or similar areas of work were grouped together. The objective here was to apply the general principles of good practice to their specific work situations. We asked each group to come up with plans for immediate and long-term changes in practice and policy which, in the light of the training day, they would now like to see.

At the end of the day we had a feedback session and asked everyone to fill in an evaluation form. The feedback we got on the evaluation sheets was overwhelmingly positive, and many stressed the usefulness of working in inter-agency groups. Many people also commented positively on the way the day was structured and the way workshop leaders had facilitated discussion. We consider this a compliment to and a recognition of feminist working methods. Not only do we have our analysis, knowledge and expertise based on years of working on these issues, but also an understanding of group processes which facilitate learning and changing. What was also acknowledged was the massive need for further training. These are just a few of the comments from the evaluation forms:

> 'Supportive, motivating, inspiring – gave hope for the future' . . . 'Very informative and interesting day – the first of many, I hope' . . . 'This experiential learning is very useful, small group discussion ideal for the topic' . . . 'Honest, supportive sharing of ideas' . . . 'Made me aware of agencies I never knew existed' . . . 'Gave us a lot to think about, has made me more aware of all the issues and more well informed' . . . 'It was a very positive day which left me feeling hopeful, but also angry that enough is not good enough, in terms of our agency's response!' . . . 'Very enlightening, if harrowing at times. I found I had to come to terms with some very uncomfortable feelings and emotions – thank you! . . . 'Thank you for a most rewarding day – it's good to know you're not "alone".'

One of the foremost concerns of the day was child sexual abuse and 'the right' approach to it. Although we had pointed out early on that there are no easy solutions to the problem of sexual violence, we constantly encountered requests for a blueprint response as well as a professional reflex of wanting to refer the problem on, especially to social services. In turn, the social workers present stressed their desperate need for resources, specialist workers, support networks, further training and alternatives to taking children into care.

The responses of teachers at the training day highlight the problems we foresee if feminists do not get more involved in training. Most of the teachers present saw their problem as not knowing how to detect abuse. They therefore wanted to be told what 'the signs' of abuse are. Whilst we know there are a range of behavioural changes which *might* indicate that a child is being or has been abused, we also know that for some children who are being systematically abused, school is the only place where they feel safe and hence are unlikely to manifest detectable 'signs'. They are likely to be perceived as the classic 'good pupil', and therefore presumed to have no problems. Their abuse will remain hidden if training for teachers focuses only on detecting abuse via a catalogue of 'symptoms'. Training should aim to encourage the creation of environments in which children feel able to disclose. Furthermore, the training must address detailed policy as to what should be done once a child has disclosed abuse. We found that most teachers had not thought through the implications of the decision on whether to make a formal report. Even fewer teachers had considered that there may well be child sexual abuse occurring within the school itself, both by peers and by adults. Our suggestion that the issue of sexual harassment should be taken up in schools was initially met with a stunned silence.

This failure to work through what tackling child sexual abuse involves has implications for any prevention work in schools. In some schools brief prevention sessions are conducted at assembly, or videos are shown, without any preparatory training for the teaching and ancillary staff. Such ill-thought-out presentations can have a number of unintended negative consequences, ranging from teachers making inappropriate jokes or comments, through to their feeling unable to deal with children's questions and concerns. We think that local education authorities should see it as a priority to provide resources both to develop and monitor prevention work in schools and to ensure that teachers and ancillary staff get the training they need in order to respond to children adequately.

Whilst our first training project was successful, it merely highlighted for us the necessity for feminists to get involved in this work and claim our status as experts. In the current climate training is being demanded by a wide variety of professional and voluntary groups. If feminists do not respond, the complexities of our analysis and understanding will not be part of the process of change that is currently underway, especially in relation to child sexual abuse. Norwich Consultants are planning a further inter-agency training day on the short- and long-term effects of sexual violence, and we will also offer in-depth specialist training for particular groups and organizations on request.

On a wider level what we have learnt in Norwich from the last two years is that there are ways in which we can create the impetus for change by encouraging local government to take up the issue of sexual violence. This hasn't been achieved by paid workers or an initiative from a radical council, but by activists from a number of grassroots feminist organizations combining and working together with the Equal Opportunities Officer.

Finally, in working together some of the excitement we experienced when we first got involved in activism has returned. As we break out of the specialisms that have developed in feminist services for abused women and girls, we are challenging, supporting and learning from each other as we take on new areas of work. We are addressing longstanding concerns in a new and more complex way, and gaining a wider and more inclusive understanding of the entire continuum of male sexual violence. Perhaps most importantly, by working together we are much more able to combine the feminist service work of our separate organizations with campaigning and work for genuine social change.

Reference

WOMEN'S COMMISSION (1986) *Violence Against Women* London: Cabinet Office.

ISLINGTON SOCIAL SERVICES: Developing a Policy on Child Sexual Abuse

Margaret Boushel and Sara Noakes

This policy seeks to protect sexually abused children from further abuse by exploring within the context of the Child Care Policy how their non-abusing family or family networks may be enabled to offer protection without the necessity of the child coming into care. Only if protection within these non-abusing networks cannot be provided should statutory action to protect the child be considered. (Report to Islington Social Services and Health Committee, 10 September 1987)

Local authorities have a statutory responsibility to protect children from abuse and neglect. The law pertaining to this responsibility is complicated, confusing and sometimes inadequate. Individual local authorities therefore sometimes develop local policy and practice guidelines for social workers and other social services staff clarifying their interpretation of the law and their expectations of workers' practice.

In Islington, an inner-city borough in North London, policy guidelines on non-accidental injury to children were, until recently, mainly geared to dealing with physical abuse. We were unprepared for the sudden emergence of so many sexual abuse cases. Not only was there no policy on how to deal with them, but social workers had also not had the opportunity to develop confidence and experience in this area. We also lacked a coherent theoretical model from which to start. Many of us felt uncomfortable with the family dysfunction model but did not know what the alternatives might be. At best, this left us feeling panic-stricken and overwhelmed when coping with sexual abuse and suspicion of abuse. At worst, it could lead to avoidance and denial of the abuse and the erosion of the valuable skills that women had developed in working with other women in a supportive way.

About three years ago one woman in the Islington Social Services Department took the initiative in tackling these issues and sent an open letter around the department inviting interested workers to get together to do some work on them. From that meeting a small group was formed to develop policy and practice guidelines, while others decided to concentrate on training and other issues.

In developing the policy we had to acknowledge both the constraints and the power we have as workers in the statutory sector. To the worker making the difficult decision to remove a child from home, a clear theoretical perspective on abuse and abusers is essential, as is an awareness that reception into care, particularly if close links with family and community are not maintained, can be an extremely painful and destructive experience for the child. Our statutory powers also bring us face to face with our own and society's expectations and understanding of the position of women as mothers and their ability and/or willingness to protect their children. We think that a policy which underlines the importance of working alongside the child's mother and non-abusing family members to help them provide protection within their own network is the most positive approach to dealing with these dilemmas. It encourages practice which is both feminist and child-centred.

The policy also attempts to deal with issues around race and culture in a way that is not prescriptive – that is, Bengali families will react like this, Afro-Caribbean families will react like that – but does acknowledge that disclosing sexual abuse may have different repercussions in a community because of cultural differences and because we live in a racist society. It is the statutory worker's responsibility to be sensitive to this without being immobilized by it.

To protect children and to try to prevent their removal from home we believe that working closely with the police is essential in child sexual abuse cases. The policy advocates involving the Police Juvenile Bureau at an early stage and also states that a named abuser should not be confronted without police being present. We want to ensure that police evidence is not destroyed or abusers forewarned, while being sensitive to the possible trauma to the child. The policy and discussions resulting from it have led to a procedure for inter-agency co-operation between the police, the health authority and social services for dealing with medical examinations that will, we hope, also contribute to lessening the trauma for the child involved.

Printed below is the Introduction to the Policy and Practice Guidelines we have developed. The guidelines go on to advise in some detail the approach to be taken by workers in the department when dealing with suspicion, disclosure, securing the immediate protection of the child, convening a case conference and creating a longer-term protection plan for a child who has been abused or is suspected of being abused. The aim is to protect the child by removing the abuser where possible and to enlist the mother's support in doing this, while recognizing the great difficulties this may pose for her.

These Policy and Practice Guidelines were the subject of extensive consultation within the department and amongst other local agencies such as the police, health and education authorities and minority ethnic and voluntary organizations. Other agencies are developing guidelines stemming from the policy for workers within their own departments. Detailed discussions are taking place with the police and health and education authorities in order to ensure a coherent inter-agency approach to child sexual abuse work within the borough. The Guidelines were presented to the Social Services Committee in September 1987 and have been agreed as council policy.

Getting this far has demanded a great deal of work, time and patience from the small group involved. Contrary to our fears, however, we have found that when presented with proposals backed up by some knowledge of current research and grounded in an awareness of good childcare practice and the department's needs, both departmental management and councillors on the Social Services Committee have been positive about the work undertaken and the end result.

A lot more work remains to be done. For the policy to become practice, extensive training is needed for social workers, children's day-care workers and residential workers. On a more general level, changes in the law and court procedure need to be pursued to ensure that children's evidence is dealt with sensitively and given the weight it deserves. The debate needs to be developed around whether an older child – and perhaps particularly a child from an ethnic minority – should have choices about the involvement of the police. More research is needed around whether any work with abusers can be effective in preventing further abuse. This is a crucial issue for social workers in trying to plan for a child's future. Lastly, as feminists we urgently need to develop the debate around our expectations of women as mothers, and our rights, choices and responsibilities in that role.

Islington Town Hall

SOCIAL SERVICES DEPARTMENT

Child Sexual Abuse – Policy and Practice Guidelines

1   Introduction

1.1   'Child Sexual Abuse is . . . the involvement of developmentally immature children and adolescents in sexual actions . . . which they cannot fully comprehend, to which they cannot give informed consent, and which violate the social taboos of family roles.' (Kempe and Kempe, 1978)

'The damaging factor is not the blood tie, but rather the betrayal of trust by a person in a position of power over the child.' (Incest Survivors Campaign 1984)

The key elements of any definition of child sexual abuse are:
1 Betrayal of trust and responsibility;
2 Abuse of power for the sexual gratification of the abuser;
3 Inability of children to consent.

1.2   These guidelines provide a framework for all those who work with children on how to recognise child sexual abuse and how to deal with it in a way that supports and protects the child. They do not lessen the importance and need for a sensitive assessment and response to each child's particular situation.

In cases where the guidelines are not followed, the reasons should be clearly recorded.

1.3   These guidelines should be read within the context of the Department's Child Care Policy. The aim is the same – to prevent Reception into Care by every means possible and, if Reception into Care is necessary in the interests of the child, to enable her/him to maintain her/his links with family and community networks. Family and community networks are, however, interpreted as the *non-abusing* family and networks. This is developed within these Child Sexual Abuse policy and practice guidelines by the emphasis on working with and trying to support the non-abusing parent (usually the mother) to enable her to protect the child.

These guidelines also develop the Child Care Policy by making clear circumstances in which it is *not* in the child's interests to remain at home, viz:
– where the named abuser continues to live with the family.

In addition they clarify the Child Care Policy on issues of access and rehabilitation by stating that:

(a) the named abuser should not, so far as we can make it possible, have unsupervised access to the child;

(b) any plan for rehabilitation involving the named abuser should be developed with a great deal of caution and include safeguards for the child.

With Child Sexual Abuse work as with other childcare work, clear planning, time-limited objectives and shared care and decision-making with non-abusing parents are essential.

1.4   It is clear that child sexual abuse is common. Current research indicates that about 20% of girls and 10% of boys will have been sexually abused as children.* Child sexual abuse is not concentrated in any particular class or ethnic group. It is also clear from the research that children do not falsely report abuse. The difficulty they have is in talking about it at all, or sometimes in naming the abuser. Where the abuser is a family member feelings of loyalty and a need to trust may make it particularly difficult for the child to speak.

1.5   Most abusers are men and many are in a relationship of trust and authority to the victim. In one sample 94% of sexually abused girls and 84% of sexually abused boys were abused by men. In the same sample, 50% of the girls and 17% of the boys were abused by a family member. Abusers of both boys and girls are more likely to be heterosexual men than homosexual men.

Only a very small proportion of abusers are women (about 3% of the total). In many of these situations there is more than one abuser involved.

1.6   Research so far has not produced a coherent explanation as to why abusers are predominantly men and why they abuse. No single clear factors have emerged that distinguish abusers from non-abusers. Male abusers in general do not seem to suffer from any recognised psychiatric or personality disorders.

There are also no adequate studies to evaluate treatment programmes and the likelihood of abusers re-offending.* Workers therefore need to be very cautious about any rehabilitation plans that involve the abuser.

1.7   Sexual abuse does not always cause obvious physical injury. However, physical damage may occur, e.g., genital cuts, warts, bruises and infections, pregnancy. Psychological damage without obvious physical damage is more common. This may include sleeping and eating disturbances, depression, self-injury, drug abuse etc. (see Appendix A). Often a child's behaviour is the major clue that abuse is taking place.

1.8   Unless the abuse is stopped and the child is given help it is clear from all the research that the child may be psychologically damaged for the rest of her/his life, e.g., may suffer from low

* All references are to *Child Sexual Abuse – A source Book*, D. Finklehor (Collier McMillan), which provides a most comprehensive and up-to-date review of current research.

self-esteem, self-destructive behaviour, mental health problems and difficulties in developing close trusting relationships. The extent of the long-term damage caused by sexual abuse is related to four main factors:

1 How much the child trusted or expected to be able to trust the person who abused her/him;
2 How long the abuse carried on;
3 To what extent physical force or intimidation was used;
4 How well the child was believed, helped and protected when the abuse was discovered.

1.9 These guidelines do not accept the idea that mothers are to blame if their children are abused.

It is the abuser who is responsible for the abuse. It is common for a child to feel that her/his mother knew that the abuse was happening, workers should not assume that this is so.

It is very important for the child's recovery, especially when the abuser is a family member, that every effort is made to build and strengthen the relationship with the mother. This can be difficult.

A mother's first reaction may be shock, disbelief and even anger with the child – reactions similar to the early stages of bereavement (where the abuser is outside the family, both parents may react this way).

In some situations it may take a mother considerable time to work through her feelings. Her own past experiences, fears of violence from the abuser, ambivalent feelings towards the abuser, having to face losing her relationship with the abuser and the difficulties involved in this separation are some of the reasons which may contribute to a mother being unable either to acknowledge the abuse or protect her child.

The worker needs to acknowledge and be sensitive to these feelings. The child's welfare and protection must be the first consideration of all staff. To achieve this it is the social worker's responsibility to protect and work with the child's mother to help strengthen her ability to support her child in the longer term, even if she cannot offer such protection immediately.

1.10 Child sexual abuse happens in all cultures and all children have a right to be protected. Cultural differences must not be used as a reason for non-intervention, but workers should not ignore family and community networks as a source of protection.

Workers should be sensitive to the many differing factors which may need to be taken into consideration depending on a child's racial or cultural background, for example:

- it may be more difficult for a black child to disclose to representatives of white authority that s/he has been abused – the consequences for the family might be quite different than for a white family
- it may be that the child has internalised racism or other negative cultural stereotypes in a way that makes her/him feel that s/he has been abused because of her colour/religion etc.
- religious and cultural beliefs may exacerbate feelings of shame and guilt
- it may be less easy for a mother to protect her child in some cultures than in others, depending on the power position of women within their culture
- it may be that the consequences of disclosing within a particular culture are that the abused child will never be accepted back into her/his community.

It may be that workers will need to consult with appropriate ethnic minority colleagues and/or the Ethnic Minority Specialist Workers on these issues.

1.11 Some children are more vulnerable to abuse, e.g. if physical disability makes them dependent on adults for a high degree of primary care, or if learning disability means they are less well able to understand and communicate what has happened to them. Because these children are more dependent on their carers, disclosure may also be more practically and emotionally difficult for them.

1.12 These guidelines are geared to adult/child abuse. Where children are being abused by other children, decisions on what action to take must take into account the following factors:
(a) the power relationship between the children;
(b) the ability of adult carers to protect;
(c) that the young abuser may be displaying sexualised behaviour as a result of having been abused himself/herself.
Workers should consider whether a Child Abuse Case Conference is necessary.

1.13 Police (Juvenile Bureau) should be informed at an early stage, in all cases of child sexual abuse. Police Care Officers will then have to inform C.I.D. because of the nature of the offence.

Even in cases where a carer is able and willing to protect a child from further abuse, police should be involved in case other children are at risk either now or in the future.

Police are able to investigate the offence more effectively than Social Services and to establish:
1 What evidence there is for prosecution;
2 If there is evidence to remove the abuser, rather than the child;

3 If there is more than one abuser;

4 If there is more than one victim.

A police investigation gives a clear message to the child and abuser that the child has a right not to be abused.

Note

The work on developing and drafting Islington's policy was largely undertaken by Margaret Boushel, Wendy Holmes, Joa Luke, Sara Noakes and Sue Stewart, all of whom work in Islington Social Services Department. We have had lots of support and advice from Mary MacLeod and Esther Saraga and other friends and colleagues.

DEVELOPING A FEMINIST SCHOOL POLICY ON CHILD SEXUAL ABUSE

Maureen O'Hara

Teachers are one of the most important potential sources of support for children who are being sexually abused. This is so particularly if the abuser is living in the child's home and she feels unable to talk to others in her family about the abuse. A small number of schools now have policies aimed at offering children support and a means of escape from sexual abuse. In many other schools there are teachers who want to offer support to children but who are unsure about how to do so. Where that is the case, feminist teachers can have a powerful impact on the kind of policy a school develops, especially when the head and senior teachers are basically sympathetic to 'equal opportunities' policies. A policy on sexual abuse is likely to be effective only in schools where pupils feel there is a genuine commitment to challenging sexism, racism and class oppression, since it is only then that *all* pupils can begin to trust teachers enough to talk about abuse. Schools where there is a high level of solidarity amongst at least a core of women staff are obviously more likely to develop a feminist policy.

I taught at a special school (for pupils with emotional and behavioural difficulties – an 'EBD' school) which developed a policy from a basically feminist perspective. This was easier to do than it would have been in a mainstream school, mainly because of the small number of staff and pupils in special schools. Another important factor was that it was the type of school in which all members of staff, including nonteaching staff, were able to have some influence over school policy. However, similar policies could be developed in mainstream schools where enough staff are interested. I am trying to introduce a similar policy at the comprehensive where I now work, and so far I've had a very positive response.

How the policy came about

Women at the school had started meeting separately from the rest of the staff, mainly to discuss strategies for dealing with the high level of sexual harassment of girls and women by boys in the school. The issue of sexual harassment had galvanized the women, none of whom saw themselves as feminists except for me. Discussion within the women's group about this issue led on to the issue of sexual violence in general, and to the idea of developing school policies which challenged violence against girls and women. At around the same time the issue of child sexual abuse became very immediate because of the circumstances of one of the pupils. After about three weeks of pressure from women staff, a meeting of the entire staff was arranged to discuss sexual abuse. I offered to write a discussion paper on sexual abuse which would include suggestions for a school policy. Most of the policy suggestions were agreed on by all the staff at the meeting, mainly because of the arguments put forward by the women's group.

The elements of the policy

There are basically two aspects to developing an effective policy. On the one hand there needs to exist an atmosphere in which pupils can have some trust in the willingness of teachers to believe and support them if they disclose abuse. On the other hand, individual teachers and the school as an institution need to be clear about how to respond if a pupil does disclose abuse.

A school policy on sexual abuse obviously can't exist in isolation from the total school environment. If pupils' experience of teachers is that they generally take their feelings and opinions seriously, they are more likely to trust teachers' commitment to protecting them from sexual abuse. The school's attitude to verbally or physically abusive behaviour towards or among pupils is crucial to developing an effective policy (see Whitbread, 1980, for a discussion of the development of a school policy on sexual harassment). If pupils feel protected from sexual and racial harassment and assault, as well as from general bullying within the school, they are more likely to trust the school's ability to protect them from abuse taking place outside the school. The more pupils have participated in discussions about the content of antisexist and antiracist policies, particularly in relation to harassment and assault, the more they will take seriously the teacher's commitment. The policies themselves will be much more effective if they have an input from pupils.

It is also vital that teachers are aware that sexual abuse is universal, and that it occurs in equal porportions in all social groups, cutting across economic, racial, regional and other divisions. Classist and racist stereotypes about sexual abuse are widespread and need to be challenged as part of the process of developing a policy. When the true extent of sexual abuse is acknowledged its links with other forms of sexual violence also become clearer.

The importance of sex education

The type of sex education which takes place within the school is also crucial. Much of the sex education currently taught in schools is, for girls and young women, little more than training in the sexual servicing of men, with some information about reproduction and contraception. Discussion of female sexuality is virtually nonexistent in schools, as is any positive discussion of lesbianism or homosexuality.[1] It is still rare to find a sex education programme which mentions the existence of the clitoris. Girls are generally given the impression that their 'sex organs' consist of their vagina and ovaries together (it's rare to see a diagram of one without the other).

The kind of sex education which can most effectively challenge sexual abuse takes the potential for a positive, autonomous female sexuality as its starting point. The central focus is not on an individual's actual or potential relationships with others, but on her feelings about herself. (Good sources for work with young women around sexuality are Meulenbelt, 1981; Myles *et al.*, 1985.) If young women know their own bodies and are in touch with their own sexual feelings, they have more potential for making genuine choices about their sexual relationships. They are also better equipped to resist coercion and exploitation. If sexuality is discussed in ways which clearly distinguish between sexual exploitation and relationships based on equality and mutual consent, and which recognize the rights of both children and adults to defend themselves against abuse, children will feel supported. Even if they do not disclose abuse, the acknowledgement of their rights and a clear statement that the responsibility for any form of sexual abuse lies with the abuser can have a very positive effect on a child's self-esteem. This kind of sex education will be much more effective if provision is made in mixed schools for single-sex teaching. This is also important in developing trust between girls and women teachers.

Confidentiality

One of the most difficult issues for teachers trying to support children who are being sexually abused is deciding whether to take any action, such as informing social services, which is against the child's expressed wishes. This question is not likely to arise with younger children, but with adolescents the situation is much more complex. Particularly if the police and courts are involved, intervention often results in what amounts to secondary abuse. Whether this is the case depends in large part on the policies and procedures of the local social services department and on the relationship they have with the police. There is no solution to conflicts over confidentiality which applies to every individual but I think it is absolutely essential never to give the child the impression that a confidence will be respected if that is not the case. It is best to avoid a situation in which an adult is party to a shared secret, as in some ways this replicates the child's experience of abuse. One way of improving the level of support for children would be for feminist teachers, social workers and others working with children and young women to link up with each other.

Main points of the written policy

All pupils who inform members of staff about their experiences of sexual abuse should be believed.

The responsibility for the abuse should clearly be seen to lie with the abuser. It should in no way be implied to the child or to non-abusing members of her family that they have any responsibility for the abuse.

In all cases our starting point should be the child – that is, the protection of the child from further abuse and emotional support for that child. This should take absolute precedence over any concern for the abuser.

Every possible attempt should be made to create a basis of emotional support for the child with non-abusing members of her family. Particular emphasis should be placed on strengthening the child's relationship with her mother where possible, and supporting the mother in confronting the abuser. (As a special school with its own social workers we were in a position to try to do this. Some social services departments have a similar policy as a result of the work of feminist social workers.)

All children should be informed of the options open to them in dealing with the abuse. They should be given emotional and practical support in making their own choices as far as possible.

It should be suggested to girls who inform staff of sexual abuse that they talk to a woman staff member if they have not already done so.

In order to create an atmosphere in which pupils feel able to seek support, sexual abuse should be discussed within the sex education programme in such a way that children's right to defend their physical and emotional integrity is clearly recognized. All girls should be told about the existence of Rape Crisis centres and incest Survivors' groups.

Obviously, the existence of a written policy is no guarantee that it will be put into practice. It will work only to the extent that teachers are committed to making it work. Its existence does, however, give committed teachers legitimacy with other teachers, and it makes it more likely that the staff as a whole will be more sensitive about sexual abuse. As with any such policy, it is a means by which pressure can be exerted rather than an assurance that sexual abuse will be dealt with in a supportive way.

Notes

Maureen O'Hara has been involved in campaigns against violence against women for several years. Since she began teaching she has been particularly active in educational and campaign work opposing the sexual abuse of children.

I would like to thank Linda Stepulevage for helping me to clarify some of the ideas in this article.

1 See GEN (March 1987) available from Women's Education Resource Centre, ILEA Drama and Tape Centre, Princeton Street, London WC1R 4BH.

References

MEULENBELT, Anja (1981) *For Ourselves* London: Sheba Feminist Publishers.

MYLES, *et al.* (1985) *Taught Not Caught: Strategies for Sex Education* Cambridge: Learning Development Aids.

SPENDER, Dale and SARAH, Elizabeth (1980) *Learning to Lose: Sexism and Education* London: The Women's Press.

WHITBREAD, Ann (1980) 'Female Teachers Are Women First: Sexual Harassment at Work' in SPENDER and SARAH (1980).

'PUTTING IDEAS INTO THEIR HEADS': Advising the Young

Jane Cousins Mills

Over ten years ago when researching my sex education book for teenagers, *Make It Happy*, I decided early on that it should be the teenagers themselves who would decide what went into it. Incest and paedophilia (although few used these actual words) were two subjects which they spontaneously raised and insisted I should not ignore. Not one of the many sex educators, child psychologists, parents, doctors and others in the childcaring professions whom I consulted raised the subject of child sexual abuse.

Much has changed in the intervening years. The professionals are now openly writing and talking about child sexual abuse. It is no longer only the feminist bookshops which stock books on the subject. However, one thing hasn't changed. The paragraphs in my book – I now believe them to be all too brief – explaining merely what the words mean, the legal position and where to get help, have attracted and continue to attract more angry criticism from the moral right than anything else that is mentioned. I have been accused of 'putting ideas into children's heads before they are ready' and of 'teaching vulnerable young children that adult–child sex is normal'. I now see that the initial silence from the professionals and the subsequent fury from those who wish to impose ignorance on all children was and is all part of what Dr Marietta Higgs of Cleveland has discovered:

> 'I think what is happening to me, and all the anger that is directed against me, is a direct analogy of what happens to children when they disclose that they have been abused or when abuse is detected.'

The breaking of the taboo on speaking out about this taboo (and just how taboo is something that is clearly so prevalent?) is largely due to the women's movement and to the brave persistence of women who have refused to keep men's secrets any longer. This silencing of women has been an age-old weapon of patriarchal society, nowhere more eloquently revealed than in Maya Angelou's *I Know Why the Caged Bird Sings*. (This was first published in 1969 in the USA; we had to wait until 1984 for it to be published in the UK.) The adolescent Maya was literally unable to speak for months after she had been raped by her mother's lover who was subsequently murdered by her uncles, thus increasing her sense of guilt for even mentioning it.

In 1978 Louise Armstrong published the first ever testimonies of women who had been sexually abused, including her own, in *Kiss Daddy Goodnight: A Speak-out On Incest*. Her US paperback publishers market this immensely brave and powerful book with disgusting, almost titillating hype: 'A shocking, challenging exposé of our ultimate sexual taboo!' is blazoned across the cover with a photo of an attractive young miss in braids and school uniform whose vulnerable looks brand her as 'victim'. Her appearance is one which is aped in pornographic books and brothels the world over. But in the women's testimonies nothing can shake the overwhelming sense of honesty, an angry insistence upon breaking the taboo of silence and, most of all, a determination to survive. Owing everything to a feminist conscious-ness, research method and style, Armstrong's book both exposes and provides a basis for analysis of the abuse of power perpetrated by adult men on (mostly) female children.

More women added their voices to a growing bibliography offering analysis, support and suggestions for prevention and change. The psychoanalyst Alice Miller began her attack on what she terms 'poison-ous pedagogy' in 1979. By this she means the way in which parents project their own fantasies and desires on their offspring, producing children who are coerced into pleasing parents who need to break their wills. In 1981 she published an all-out attack on Freud's theory of infantile sexuality in *Thou Shalt Not be Aware*. Florence Rush, an American psychiatric social worker, had come to the same conclusion in 1980 in *The Best Kept Secret: Sexual Abuse of Children*. Combining an historical assessment with personal testimony and a perceptive femi-nist critique of society, Rush lucidly reveals how Freudian theory has been used to support a patriarchal society which eroticizes the image of little girls and then blames the victims for being seductive.

Most of the (mainly male) professional studies by psychologists had presented a very different picture from that of Miller and Rush, as Elizabeth Ward in *Father–Daughter Rape* catalogues: 'the men come across as peculiarly passive: they are like helpless dolls being manipu-lated by their wives, their daughters, their mothers' (Ward, 1984). The highly dangerous myths about colluding mothers, seductive girls who lie about non-existent rape experiences and powerless men continued to underpin the so-called 'official' reports. One basic fact was ignored except by the abused and by feminist writers such as Toni A. H. McNarron and Yarrow Morgan in *Voices in the Night: Women Speaking*

About Incest: the men who are often weakly ineffectual when confronted by authority outside the home abuse their power over young children using brutal physical and/or psychological strength in the safety of their own homes.

The starting point for the long – and often confused – debate that has taken place about Freudian theory of infantile sexuality is Freud's admission of a change in mind about paternal seduction:

> Almost all my women patients told me that they had been seduced by their fathers. I was driven to recognize in the end that these reports were untrue and so came to understand that the hysterical symptoms are derived from phantasies and not from real occurrences. (Freud, 1966)

The key text from Alice Miller was her belief that 'children will produce pseudo-sexual feelings in order to be a satisfactory partner for the frustrated parent' (Miller, 1985).

As a result most of the books aimed at young children reviewed here present them as asexual blobs of near-humanity for whom any basic sex education is unnecessary. Clearly, one of the negative legacies of a persistently patriarchal interpretation of Freudian drive theory – and one properly exposed by feminists – is the popular misconception that young girls are responsible, because of their own unconscious desires, for seducing adults. Thus the blame has been transferred from the abuser to the victim: 'Psychiatry often defines young victims as seductive and perpetrators as sick men who must be pitied, which may explain why the rape of (female) children is now much less severely punished than in the nineteenth century', Anna Clark chillingly observes in *Women's Silence, Men's Violence* (Clark, 1987).

Another negative legacy is the belief that children lie about sexual abuse. 'Believe the child' is the message that comes over loud and clear from all the books reviewed here. There is evidence that psychologists and the non-professionals alike are beginning to accept this. It may be the one most positive and enduring result of the current public debate.

A total denial of infantile sexuality seems to me to be a deeply retrogressive step. Acceptance does not have to mean the condoning of adult-child sexual activity in the cause of sexual rights for children. As Sarah Nelson writes in *Incest: Fact and Myth*, an excellent resumé of past and current misconceptions and the negative effects of both patriarchal assumptions and feminist attempts to redress the balance:

> It is possible that Freud was simply wrong about childhood incestuous fantasies . . . especially when we recall the highly dubious starting-point for the theory, his refusal to believe his patients' accounts of childhood abuse.
>
> But . . . we need not retreat into a reactionary position to question more general aspects of Freud's views on infant sexuality. We can accept that children are not some separate neuter category of humanity but are at least latently sexual beings, capable of sensual feeling and enjoyment. (Nelson, 1987)

The authors of books for teenagers on the whole achieve a better perspective than their colleagues writing for younger children. It is more generally accepted that teenagers do have sexual feelings (although I know that there are many adults who would like to deny even this.) The teenagers' books also reveal a society closer to reality than is found in the books for the young where families tend to be white, middle-class and nuclear, where fathers play virtually no role in the nurturance of the children and highly educated mothers are hugely endowed with verbal and play-acting skills and have all the time in the world to read stories to their asexual offspring.

The best of all the novels written for teenagers is the impressive first novel of Sandra Chick, *Push Me, Pull Me*, which explores the emotional confusion of a thirteen-year-old girl who is sexually abused by her stepfather. It is an honest and totally realistic portrayal of a family that has absorbed the contradictions of patriarchal society. There is no neat didactic resolution to the narrative – but rather, a positive sense that the girl is learning to be a survivor rather than a victim. The family in *Porky* by Deborah Moggach (for adults and older teenagers) is certainly not idealized either but reactionary politics in the form of a weak, misunderstood father, a colluding mother, and a daughter who is a victim, not a survivor, imbue the whole story. An unpleasant novel.

Both Richard Peck's *Are You in the House Alone?* and Sandra Scoppettone's *Happy Endings Are All Alike* were written for American teenagers about acquaintance-rape. This has come to be seen as a major concern for a generation brought up to fear only strangers. As Michele Elliott points out, this is like teaching children to cross the road but to look out only for the red cars.) Whereas Peck's novel is the sort of heavy-handed advice-disguised-as-fiction tale which most teenagers will run a mile from or feel conned by, Scoppettone's novel, which deals gently with a teenage lesbian love relationship, eschews all didacticism.

Of the non-fiction for teenagers, the best by far is Rosemary Stones's *Too Close Encounters And What To Do About Them.* No teenager – or parent – should be without it. Stones writes straight-forwardly, without a hint of condescension, in language that teenagers will both respect and learn from. The practical advice and factual information is presented in the context of an intelligent analysis of the sexist society which we all inhabit. I suppose some adults will object that it is too frank and overly non-sexist, but few teenagers will.

No Is Not Enough: Helping Teenagers Avoid Sexual Abuse by Caren Adams, Jennifer Fay and Jan Loreen-Martin is the perfect complement to Stones's book. The (American) authors cover every aspect of sexual abuse, provide support and advice for the parents of abused children

and sensible suggestions for both short- and long-term prevention. Would that it were published here, with British advice and help organizations listed, for teaching children merely how to say 'no' is *not* enough: 'We have to raise boys with more reverence for nurturance and less for violence' (Adams *et al.*, 1984). There is strong evidence which suggests that those men who are closely involved in the childcare of their children do not become abusers.

Both these last two books insist that the connexion between sexual assault and sexuality cannot be ignored. Their authors stress the need for adequate sex education if children are to learn how to respect and protect themselves. This plea can also be heard in the personal testimonies of women who subsequently realized that their ignorance had made their exploitation all the easier for the abuser. These pleas are ignored by the majority of authors for pre-teens. Most of the books have an unreal air; children are presented as if they have few or no sensual feelings and absolutely no sexual feelings – conscious or unconscious. It is not just teens who need to understand the difference between healthy sexuality and abusiveness and exploitation. If a child's first introduction to sex is in the form of discussions or stories about harmful and perverted exploitation, this will not provide the basis for secure sexual feelings in adult life – let alone during childhood and adolescence. Sex and violence are closely linked in our society:

> Violence is considered by many to be sexy, and sex often includes violence. Some of what is accepted as normal sexual behaviour actually includes some forms of sexual assault. (Adams *et al.*, 1984)

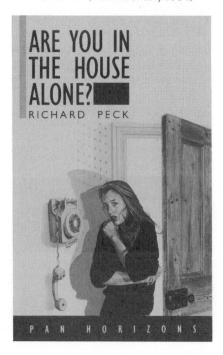

For the very young, it does make sense to talk about sexual assault in the context of protection along with advice about crossing roads, how to dial 999, what to do in a fire, and so on. It is also crucial that children learn how to value themselves and their bodies. How sensible is it to tell children that sex is about nothing other than to make babies? This can only lead to confusion and increased vulnerability when they are confronted by the fact that for most adults this is not the case. A lovely introduction to sex education for the young is Claire Rayner's *The Body Book*. It ought to offend no one. If Rayner's book is a bit heavy on the 'sex is for baby-making' line, *The Playbook for Kids About Sex* by Joani Blank is not. It is a book I have long admired but because it is so honest and frank – about masturbation, homosexuality, birth control, etc. – some adults may not be ready for it.

The first fiction book to be published in the UK aimed at young children and focusing on child sexual abuse prevention was *No More Secrets For Me* by Oralee Wachter. Four stories intended to be read aloud to four to eight-year-olds illustrate what a child's rights are, what situations might be risky, ways to prevent sexual abuse and what to do if you are abused. Many parents will learn as much as their children will. (How many adults genuinely believe that their children have any rights?) Unfortunately the book is marred by an introduction from one Dr Andrew Stanway who is not immune from several deeply sexist assumptions; for example:

> The role of men in today's world has changed so dramatically that many simply do not have sufficiently robust personalities to cope. A man . . . is under pressure at home, at work, and in bed. This beleaguered male may feel so insecure and inadequate in one or more of these fields that he ends up becoming tyrannical to his family and abusing one or more of them in some way. (Wachter, 1986)

Of this pathetic, barely veiled plea for wives and mothers to know their place as angels in the house in order to protect their children, I was reminded of something Rosemary Stones wrote:

> Some sex education books (invariably those written by men) go on about how frail the male ego is and how important it is that girls/women do not make men feel sexually rejected . . . This is a very convenient argument for men 'needing' to get their own way sexually. The best place for . . . books that put forward such nonsense is the bin. (Stones, 1987)

A much better book is *The Willow Street Kids* by Michele Elliott. These stories for the same age group take the reader through 'the bully in the park', 'the flasher', good/bad secrets and touches, the obscene telephone call and the 'should I tell?' dilemma. The tales are all based on true stories told by children to the author. That's probably why they are so good. *It's OK to Say No!* by Robin Lenett and Bob Crane is for pre-schoolers and has an introduction which all parents should read.

The thirty short stories in the book provide the opportunity for children to rehearse what they would do were they in a similar situation. This provides a gentle introduction for child and parent alike to role-acting which many, especially adults, often find embarrassing.

Michele Elliott's approach in *Keeping Safe – A Practical Guide to Talking With Children* is also concerned with prevention through teaching children to say 'no'. The different attitudes to young children (ignore all mention of sex) and to teenagers (they must know about sex) sit uncomfortably together in the one book. If young children get no adequate supportive sex education, how are the teenagers to be expected to have the knowledge to deal with potentially dangerous situations? Knowledge, that is, which isn't derived from the sexist messages of the media or the myths and misconceptions of peer-group talk. However, parents of the very young are encouraged to refer to 'the parts covered by your bathing costume'. Nor is there any attempt to encourage in parents any questioning of the sort of society in which child sexual abuse is so prevalent. Of this fear of any theory, Sarah Nelson explains gently:

> Theory decides whether you believe a girl's story . . . It shapes what you tell the tearful mother. . . . Should she be more dutiful to her incestuous

husband and give up her job and social life, or should she be less obedient and dutiful? It decides whether or not you intervene at all: is incest just a happy part of that culture and best left alone? (Nelson, 1987)

Yet another book in the 'all we need to do is teach them to say no' approach is *We Can Say No!* by David Pithers and Sarah Greene. This has two white, obviously middle-class children, a mum who takes all the risky situations in her stride and no dad in sight. It has no helpful – and necessary – introduction for parents, most of whom are clearly in need of some sort of help and advice as is recognized in some of the best books reviewed here. Most alarming of all is a colour code which enjoins children to 'Be strong! Be clever! Be careful! Be safe!' But abusers are adults who are certainly stronger and often more 'clever' than children, who are brought up to believe that adults are infinite in their wisdom.

The same problem exists for the *Kidscape Primary Kit*, an otherwise impressive and comprehensive programme for prevention for teachers of five- to eleven-year-olds, with videotape, posters for children to fill in with 'Ten Golden Rules for Good Sense Defence' and pamphlets for parents. It also includes superbly clear and concise advice to teachers

on how to use the kit, how to plan the programme, how to conduct the parents' meeting, how to plan and conduct the children's lesson(s) and some fairly good children's stories (though not nearly as good as *The Willow Street Kids* by Michele Elliott, who is the founder/director of *Kidscape*).

In a recent article in *Marxism Today*, Mary MacLeod and Esther Saraga drew attention to the main drawback in an approach to protection based on believing that prevention can be achieved merely by teaching children how to say 'no':

> But children do say 'no' – and it makes no difference, except possibly to increase the threats against them. . . . This approach carries a lot of risks, particularly for the very children whom it seeks to help. It makes children responsible for adults, and may also make abused children feel even more guilty. Sex education in schools, almost ruled out by the present government, is obviously important. And there is evidence that 'Kidscape' classes may make it easier for abused children to tell. This is important, but this is not prevention. (MacLeod and Saraga, 1987)

With this reservation, I would like to see *Kidscape* provided in all primary schools and demanded by all parents. It's the best scheme yet and as such is to be applauded.

Parenting Press, Inc., in Seattle, publish three excellent pamphlets for pre-school children and their parents which keep clear of the 'teach them to say no' approach. *It's My Body*, about good and bad touches, contains no specific references to sexual abuse but, as is pointed out in the introduction, it 'emphasizes achieving autonomy through increased initiative and a sense of mastery . . . [and] prepares young children for appropriate responses to physical assault . . . without provoking potentially damaging guilt feelings' (Freeman, 1982:). The accompanying parents' and teachers' guide, *Protect Your Children from Sexual Abuse*, by Janni Hart-Rossi, is similarly excellent in showing parents that teaching our children to say 'no' is not enough.

Something Happened and I'm Scared to Tell by Patricia Kehoe is a thoughtful pamphlet for young victims of abuse aged three to seven. It is the only book I have come across that adequately explains to the young the difference between child abuse and loving sex between adults. It will gently help rebuild the fragile self-image of the young abused child. I sincerely wish that these three slim booklets were published in Britain, as the import prices make them prohibitively expensive.

The Sexual Abuse of Children, a New Zealand booklet by Miriam Saphira for parents, teachers and social workers is also good in its insistence upon combining practical advice with a demand for a re-appraisal of patriarchal values. Saphira concludes:

> As long as we stereotype our children into aggressive, power-hungry abusers and passive, submissive objects for victimization we will not reduce the potential sexual abuse of children. We need to change our

values until there is no longer an imbalance of power . . . It is the offender who chooses the child victim, but we can make his action very difficult and at times impossible if we give our child basic survival information. (Saphira, 1985)

The saddest of all the testimonies I have read was from the father of a sexually abused and murdered child who said with bewilderment that his son had been brought up to be such a good polite child and to do whatever was asked of him. He didn't stand a chance. As Alice Miller has pointed out, parents persist in adopting a poisonous pedagogical approach to child-rearing, using the techniques of disapproving looks, rejection, threats, corporal punishment and so on to 'break' their children's obstinacy, wilfulness, defiance and exuberance. 'Children raised in this way frequently do not notice, even at an advanced age, when someone is taking advantage of them as long as the person uses a "friendly" tone of voice' (Miller, 1987)

All these books, from the best which accept that prevention cannot mean merely teaching our children to say 'no', to those which are little more than well-meaning, aim to provide children with more information than has hitherto been available. Children without such information are more vulnerable than they need be. Perhaps vulnerability is what many adults unconsciously encourage in children. Vulnerability and ignorance tend to be interpreted as innocence – a dangerous confusion which neatly bolsters an adult need to feel superior and powerful. That this is mainly a male need is shown by the facts: it is overwhelmingly men who abuse, it is (mostly) girls who are abused. As Deborah Cameron put it, in a letter to the *Guardian* newspaper:

We need to consider the components of masculine sexuality in our culture. I am thinking especially of the connexion which seems to exist for men between sexual pleasure and power. . . . The key to preventing child sex abuse, then, is to break this connexion and rethink masculinity so men no longer feel impelled to seek their kicks in extreme forms of domination. (*Guardian*, August 1987)

Note

Jane Cousins Mills wrote *Make It Happy: What Sex Is All About* in 1979 (published under the name Jane Cousins). She is currently rewriting this as *Make It Happy, Make It Safe* to take on board the issues of AIDS and child sexual abuse. It will be published by Penguin in 1988. A writer and a film-maker, she is currently making a documentary film about Jean Seberg and writing *Woman-Words*, a feminist vocabulary, to be published by Longmans and Virago Press.

References

ADAMS, Caren, FAY, Jennifer and LOREEN-MARTIN, Jan (1984) *No Is Not Enough: Helping Teenagers Avoid Sexual Abuse* California: Impact Publishers.

ANGELOU, Maya (1984) *I Know Why The Caged Bird Sings* London: Virago Press.

ARMSTRONG, Louise (1978) *Kiss Daddy Goodnight: A Speak-out On Incest* New York: Pocket Books.

BLANK, Joani (1982) *The Playbook for Kids About Sex* London: Sheba Feminist Press.

CHICK, Sandra (1987) *Push Me, Pull Me* London: The Women's Press.

CLARK, Anna (1987) *Women's Silence, Men's Violence* London & New York: Pandora Press.

COUSINS, Jane (1986) *Make It Happy: What Sex Is All About* London: Penguin.

ELLIOTT, Michele (1986) *Keeping Safe: A Practical Guide to Talking With Children* London: Bedford Square Press/NCVO.

ELLIOTT, Michele (1987) *The Willow Street Kids* London: Pan Books.

FREEMAN, Lory (1982) *It's My Body* Seattle: Parenting Press, Inc.

FREUD, Sigmund (1966) *The Complete Introductory Lectures of Psychoanalysis* New York: Norton.

KEHOE, Patricia (1987) *Something Happened and I'm Scared to Tell* Seattle: Parenting Press, Inc.

HART-ROSSI, Jani (1984) *Protect Your Child From Sexual Abuse: A Parent's Guide* Seattle: Parenting Press, Inc.

LENETT, Robin and CRANE, Bob (1986) *It's OK to Say NO!: A Parent–Child Manual for the Protection of Children* London: Thorsons.

MACLEOD, Mary and SARAGA, Esther (1987) 'Abuse of Trust' *Marxism Today*, August, pp. 10–13.

MCNARRON, Toni A. H. and MORGAN, Yarrow (1982) editors, *Voices in the Night: Women Speaking About Incest* Pittsburgh: Cleis Press.

MILLER, Alice (1985) *Thou Shalt Not Be Aware: Society's Betrayal of the Child* London: Pluto Press.

MILLER, Alice (1986) *Pictures of a Childhood* New York: Farrar, Straus & Giroux.

MILLER, Alice (1987) *For Your Own Good: Hidden Cruelty in Child-Rearing and the Roots of Violence* London: Virago Press.

MOGGACH, Deborah (1983) *Porky* London; Jonathan Cape.

NELSON, Sarah (1987) *Incest: Fact and Myth* Edinburgh: Stramullion Co-operative.

PECK, Richard (1986) *Are You in the House Alone?* London: Pan Books.

PITHERS, David and GREENE, Sarah *We Can Say NO!* London: Beaver Books, in association with National Children's Home.

RAYNER, Claire (1979) *The Body Book* London: Pan Books.

RUSH, Florence (1980) *The Best Kept Secret: Sexual Abuse of Children* New York: McGraw-Hill.

SAPHIRA, Miriam (1985) *The Sexual Abuse of Children* Auckland: Papers Inc.

SCOPPETTONE, Sandra (1978) *Happy Endings Are All Alike* New York: Dell Publishing.

STONES, Rosemary (1987) *Too Close Encounters and What to Do About Them* London: Magnet.

WARD, Elizabeth (1984) *Father-Daughter Rape* London: The Women's Press.

WACHTER, Oralee (1986) *No More Secrets For Me* London: Penguin.

CHILD SEXUAL ABUSE CRISIS LINES:
Advice for our British Readers

If you know, or suspect, that a child is being sexually abused, then Social Services social work departments have a duty to investigate and to take action to protect the child.

Advice and counselling is available from your local Rape Crisis Centre. This list is correct to the best of our knowledge. (If your town does not appear, ask Directory Enquiries or ring one of the other centres.) ChildLine (0800-1111) will offer counselling/advice to children and young people.

Rape Crisis Centres

Each centre is individually organized and completely independent.

Aberdeen	0224-575560	Cumbria (Carlisle)	0228-36500
Avon (Bristol)	0272-428331	Derby	0332-372545
Belfast	0232-249696	Dublin	0001-601470
Birmingham	021-233-2122	Edinburgh	031-556-9437
Office	021-233-2655	Essex see Grays Thurrock	
Bradford	0274-308270	Exeter	0392-30871
Brighton	0273-203770	Galway	010-35391-66747
Cardiff – see South Wales		Gloucester	0452-26770
Cambridge	0223-358314	Glasgow see Strathclyde	
Central Scotland	0324-38433	Highlands	0463-220719
Chelmsford	0245-46707	Hull	0482-29990
Canterbury	0227-450400	Inverness see Highlands	
Cleveland	0642-225787	Leamington	0926-832529
Clonmell (Co. Tipperary)	052-24111	Grays Thurrock	0375-38609
Cork	010-353-968086	Leeds	0532-440058
Coventry	0203-77229	Office	0532-441323
Croydon	01-656-5362	Leicester	0533-666666

Limerick 010-35361-41211
Liverpool 051-7277599
London 01-837-1600
 Office 01-278-3956
Luton (Helpline) 0582-33592
 Office 0582-33426
Manchester 061-228-3602
Milton Keynes 0908-670333
Nottingham 0602-410440
Norwich 0603-667687
Oxford 0865-726295
 (Women's Line)
Plymouth 0752-23584
Portsmouth 0705-669511
Peterborough 0733-40515

Reading 0734-55577
Rochdale 0706-526279
Sheffield 0742-755255
Shropshire 0952-504666
Southwark 01-639-1106
South Wales 0222-373181
Southampton 0703-229288
Strathclyde 041-221-8448
Scunthorpe 0724-853953
Swansea 0792-475243
Tyneside (Helpline) 0632-329858
 Office 0632-615317
Waterford, PO Box 57, Waterford,
 Eire
Weybridge (Dorset) 0305-772295

Feminist Review

Since 1979 **Feminist Review** has aimed to explore the diverse theoretical and strategic issues and the differing experiences of women in the struggle for a socialist-feminist future. The journal is edited by a collective of women based in London, with the help of women and groups from all over the United Kingdom.

● WHY NOT SUBSCRIBE?

All subscriptions run in calendar years. The issues for 1988 are Nos. 28, 29 and 30.

● SUBSCRIPTION RATES, 1988 (3 issues)

Individual Subscriptions

UK	£14
Overseas	£18
North America	$28

A number of reduced cost (£12 per year: UK only) subscriptions are available for readers experiencing financial hardship, e.g. unemployed, student, low-paid. If you'd like to be considered for a reduced subscription, please write to the collective, c/o the Feminist Review office

Institutional Subscriptions

UK	£35
Overseas	£40
North America	$60

Bookshop	£5.95 per copy
Back issues	£14/$28 per copy

Please note that issue 11 is no longer available unless purchased as part of complete run.

Please send one year's subscription starting with Issue Number_____

I enclose payment of_____

Please send me_____copies of back issue no._____

I enclose total payment of_____

Name:_____

Address:_____

Please return this form with payment to:
**Associated Book Publishers (UK) Ltd,
Dept J, North Way, Andover, Hants, SP10 5BE**

BACK ISSUES